SEEN IN SOLITUDE

Seen In Solitude

ROBERT KIPNISS PRINTS
FROM THE
JAMES F. WHITE COLLECTION

DANIEL PIERSOL

NEW ORLEANS MUSEUM OF ART

This publication was made possible in part by the Weinstein Gallery.

3,000 copies of this book were published in conjunction with the exhibition *Seen in Solitude: Robert Kipniss Prints from the James F. White Collection,* organized by the New Orleans Museum of Art and presented March 4 through May 14, 2006. The exhibition will be presented subsequently at the Joel and Lila Harnett Museum of Art, University of Richmond Museums, Virginia, August 24 through October 1, 2006; Orlando Museum of Art, Florida, December 10, 2006, through February 11, 2007; Marion Koogler McNay Art Museum, San Antonio, Texas, March 7 through May 2, 2007; Mississippi Museum of Art, Jackson, January through April, 2008.

Library of Congress Control Number: 2005930351
ISBN 0-89494-100-3

Designed by Michael Ledet Art & Design, Hammond, LA
Photography by Judy Cooper, New Orleans Museum of Art
Produced in cooperation with the Publications Office of the New Orleans Museum of Art,
    Wanda O'Shello, Coordinator
Typography and digital composition by Eugenie Seidenberg Delaney, North Ferrisburgh, VT
Print management by Kaye Alexander, Westford, VT
Printed and bound in Singapore by Imago.

Cover: Catalogue number 55
Page 2: Catalogue number 21 (detail)
Page 18: Robert Kipniss, Photo by Marc Weinstein

CONTENTS

FOREWORD AND ACKNOWLEDGMENTS

The New Orleans Museum of Art is proud to present *Seen In Solitude: Robert Kipniss Prints from the James F. White Collection*, the first in-depth museum retrospective of this distinguished American artist's intaglios and lithographs. This presentation underscores NOMA's continuing commitment to seek out and present to our visitors the best in art on paper by significant creators and follows recent showings such as *2005 New Orleans Triennial: A Southern Perspective on Prints*; *Visions from the Soul: The Woodcuts of Hans Friedrich Grohs*; and *From Another Dimension: Works on Paper by Sculptors*.

Robert Kipniss has gained international recognition for the beautiful impressions he has produced during his long career. These haunting, contemplative images reveal his mastery as a printmaker and draw the viewer into the mysterious world conjured in their creator's fertile imagination. The eighty-six prints in the exhibition are but a fraction of the nearly six hundred that Kipniss has created to date, but they demonstrate clearly the artist's technical and stylistic evolution as a printmaker.

Seen In Solitude is the result of the efforts and contributions of many people, all of whom deserve recognition. We are indeed grateful to James F. White, who has generously lent to the exhibition's New Orleans presentation and national tour so many works from his personal collection. Dan Piersol, our recently retired Curator of Prints and Drawings and now Deputy Director for Programs of the Mississippi Museum of Art, selected the prints for the exhibition and wrote the perceptive catalogue essay. Various members of the Museum staff provided valuable services: photographer Judy Cooper produced beautiful color transparencies of the art; curatorial assistant Liede Husband prepared texts and manuscripts, which were carefully proofread by curatorial assistant George Roland and volunteer Jean Stein; librarian Sheila Cork and volunteer Karen Harris assisted with research; volunteer Diane Walmsley accurately transcribed the interview tapes; and the commitment and skills of Publications Coordinator Wanda O'Shello, working with designer Michael Ledet, have resulted in this beautiful catalogue.

Finally, we are all indebted to the artist, Robert Kipniss, not only for his patient and unhesitating cooperation in mounting this exhibition and preparing the catalogue, but also for creating the many extraordinary images that comprise it. The New Orleans Museum of Art is indeed honored that what Robert Kipniss has created in solitude may be shared with so many in this splendid exhibition.

E. JOHN BULLARD
The Montine McDaniel Freeman Director

COLLECTOR'S STATEMENT

I am occasionally asked how it came about that I started collecting prints. And often, the follow-up questions are how was I first introduced to prints by Robert Kipniss, and how did they become the focus of my collection, now numbering more than six hundred works. I invariably reply, "youthful enthusiasm coupled with a youngster's lack of art-world social graces." This is an odd, but fairly accurate answer.

I collected my first Robert Kipniss print when I was barely out of high school and with no background in the visual arts. All of my artistic inclinations were in musical performance, playing string bass in several orchestras. By chance, I received a mailing from Fine Arts 260, a division of the Book of the Month Club, which sold framed prints in editions of 260. I have no idea how my name came to be placed on the mailing list. The first mailing had a Kipniss lithograph called *Toward the Mountain*, and I just couldn't pass it up. I was a bird watcher and hiker, and felt that I knew the place in the picture (even if it was an imagined place). I collected several other impressions by Robert from Fine Arts 260 before branching out to other sources, mainly Associated American Artists, and to a few other artists such as Luigi Lucioni and Gerald Geerlings.

The youthful lack of awareness kicked in one day during my sophomore year in college, when I decided that I wanted to collect every print made by Robert Kipniss. I had no idea how many that might entail, where to get them, or what it might cost. But, inspired by my interest, I looked up where Robert lived, and by good fortune his home was on Long Island less that fifteen miles from my own. One evening, I dropped by his home unannounced to inform him in person of my plan.

Robert, good-hearted fellow that he is, and his wife invited me in to sit and talk for a fine evening. He was kind enough to overlook my lack of social graces in favor of my obvious, if clearly untutored, enthusiasm for his work. Robert invited me to visit him at his studio in Manhattan to watch him work, learn more about prints and printmaking, and view (and collect) his earliest impressions. Every autumn from then on, when his new editions were released, I would visit Robert and obtain as many of the year's prints as I could afford. More accurately, my mother and father, who have warmly supported all my artistic endeavors with great encouragement and enthusiasm throughout my life, would often financially support me in this endeavor as well. I would repay them over the rest of the year.

Two things developed from these early yearly visits and the later more frequent ones. The first is the collection, part of which is displayed in this exhibition. The second is the true friendship between Robert and me that has lasted for decades, transcending the prints and paintings, standing on its own, and which I treasure equally.

JAMES F. WHITE

SEEN IN SOLITUDE
PRINTS BY ROBERT KIPNISS

*I never found the companion that was so
companionable as solitude. We are for the
most part more lonely when we go abroad
among men than when we stay in our
chambers. A man thinking or working is
always alone, let him be where he will be.*

HENRY DAVID THOREAU, *Walden, V, Solitude*

Fig. 1
Robert Kipniss, circa 1958
Photo by Paul Elfenbein

For over five decades, Robert Kipniss (fig. 1) has prolifically produced paintings, prints and drawings of remarkable beauty, eloquence and refinement. During that time, he has gained international recognition for his distinctly American images of spacious landscapes and small town vistas, as well as quiet interiors and intimate still lifes. Following in the footsteps of such esteemed predecessors as Paul Cezanne (1839-1906) and Giorgio Morandi (1890-1964), the artist has faithfully investigated and reexamined these familiar, humble subjects over the course of his career. He never has felt confined or restricted by their narrow range; rather, he is liberated within it. To be sure, Kipniss's art has always clearly bespoken his independent spirit and lifelong embrace of solitude.

Born in Brooklyn in 1931 to Samuel and Stella Kipniss, he was afforded access to artist's materials and enthusiastically drew from his early years. His father was a layout director who designed the pages of the Sears, Roebuck & Company catalogue, while his mother was a

1

fashion illustrator. As a child, the artist sometimes accompanied his father on plein-air sketching trips outside the city. Further, Kipniss recalls spending much of his childhood living near and playing in wooded areas in the Long Island and, later, Forest Hills homes where the family lived. These solitary episodes in the outdoors unleashed his imagination, and through them he developed an abiding spiritual link to nature.

The young Kipniss was a bright but indifferent public school student. Doubtlessly his lackluster grades were the result, to a considerable extent, of his stubborn resistance to taking at face value the advice of others. Drawing, along with reading and playing pool, were his pursuits of choice during his high school years. (The artist recalls that despite his grades, he was accepted at Wittenberg College (now Wittenberg University), in

Fig. 2
Robert Kipniss (American, born 1931)
Intimations of the North Country, 1950
Private Collection, courtesy of Weinstein Gallery, San Francisco

Springfield, Ohio, in 1948 after placing in the top one percentile in the entrance examination.) In 1947, his mother, trying to steer him toward some purposeful direction, encouraged her son to take Saturday life drawing classes at the Art Students League in New York. He agreed to this, but refused to take instruction from the teacher, Alice Murphy (1896-1966). She, in turn, arranged for the lad to attend a class that met without an instructor, and thus allowed him to learn figure drawing through his own trial-and-error approach.

At Wittenberg, where he matured and gained much personal autonomy, Kipniss became serious about his studies and expanded his range of intellectual inquiry. He began composing poetry and contemplated a career as a writer. Further, his interest in cinema grew stronger through the influence of his roommate, French exchange student Pierre Lhomme (born 1930), who introduced him to European film and the work of directors such as Marcel Carné (1909-1996), Jean Renoir (1894-1979) and Jean Cocteau (1889-1963).[1]

In 1950 Kipniss transferred to the University of Iowa, and there continued his pursuit of literature and writing. He also enrolled in a painting course after reaching an agreement with professor Stuart Edie (1908-1974) that allowed him to attend classes without receiving instruction, but with the stipulation that he would accept being failed should his progress be judged inadequate. Clearly, the aspiring painter concurred with Francisco Goya's (1746-1828) heartfelt belief about art instruction that the ". . .

tyranny that obliges everyone . . . to study in the same way or to follow the same method is a great impediment to the young who practice this very difficult art . . ."[2] Kipniss's output proved, however, to be prodigious and ever more accomplished. In 1951 he entered a national painting competition at the Joe Gans Gallery in New York City and, as a result, was awarded a solo exhibition. The works displayed in that showing, with their vigorous, bravura brushwork and evocative titles such as *Mid Country* (1950) or *Intimations of the North Country* (1950) (fig. 2), reveal not only their young *auteur's* source of inspiration in the landscape but also the powerful influence of Abstract Expressionism.

Two years later Kipniss again showed in New York, now at the Harry Salpeter Gallery, but by this time he had turned decidedly away from biomorphic abstraction. As his aesthetic focus developed, he found himself drawn ever more to representational images. The new, clearly recognizable landscapes and still lifes were lauded by critic Lawrence Campbell, who remarked of a Kipniss oil that " . . . it is as though the art of painting were being rediscovered."[3]

The next several years following these early exhibitions proved to be difficult for the artist in no small measure because, as he recalls, his depictions of traditional subjects were not eagerly received by art dealers then in the thrall of the New York School and its Abstract Expressionist disciples. After graduating from the University of Iowa in 1954, he returned to New York City. There he painted every day, and every six months he made the rounds of the city's galleries with fresh canvases in hand, but to no avail. From 1956 to 1958 Kipniss served in the United States Army at bases in Texas and Virginia, painting nights and weekends in modest off-base apartments. Two more visits to New York galleries during this time also came to naught. But following his military discharge in 1958 he painted while collecting unemployment insurance, and found a receptive dealer in Karl Lunde (born 1931) at the Contemporaries gallery. A solo show there in 1959 was successful and the painter, anticipating steady sales, quit his employment as the evening manager of a bookshop. This proved to be a miscalculation, however, and he subsequently was forced to find work again, this time a position on the evening shift at the United States Post Office.

For the next few years Kipniss continued, as had been his wont, to work by night and paint by day (when he was fresh), make the occasional sale of a painting and somehow get by. Not surprisingly, this practice had become increasingly difficult. Things came dramatically to a head one fateful day in 1963 when the artist, faced with a forced move to a day position at the post office, abruptly resigned. He went to Lunde to discuss strategies to increase his exposure and sales, but a disagreement ensued and the dealer terminated his relationship with the painter. As fortune would have it, several hours later a private dealer named Muriel Werner (1924-1986) contacted Kipniss and expressed interest in handling his work. Soon she was able to sell his canvases to clients steadily enough that by the end of the year, he was able to work in his atelier full-time. By 1964, though she had enjoyed great success with his work, Werner felt that the painter's career would be furthered by the greater exposure offered by a gallery and selflessly directed him to Murray Roth (1909-1970) (fig. 3) at FAR Gallery. Roth proved a loyal and supportive champion of Kipniss's work, and an appreciative audience among critics and collectors grew steadily, along with the sales of his art.

After so much struggle and hardship, Kipniss at last was able to realize his ambition of self-sufficiency through his art. But while he now envisioned furthering his career solely through easel painting, Roth had another idea, one that would have profound and positive consequences for the artist's career. The dealer encouraged Kipniss to pursue printmaking, but the artist's initial reaction to this suggestion was less than sanguine.

Fig. 3
Robert Kipniss and Murray Roth
at FAR Gallery, New York, 1968
Photo by Leon Sokolsky

> I was resistant. The whole concept was repugnant. Working with metal, acid and various other chemicals, as well as with those strange tools, seemed much too indirect. And how could I bring my visceral experience of warm paint and welcoming canvas to a world of cold copper plates and hard steel tools?[4]

But in 1967, at Roth's insistence, the painter enrolled in an evening printmaking course taught at the Pratt Graphic Center, then located in Greenwich Village. Kipniss investigated various intaglio processes and, much to his surprise, found them to be rewarding and exciting. (Intaglio prints are those in which image areas are cut below the surface directly with a tool or by the corrosive effects of acid. The prepared plate is covered with ink and wiped by the printer, who then places a dampened sheet over the plate and rolls the combination through his press.) Soon Associated American Artists, which published artists' prints, began to represent his graphic work, and through that organization he met noteworthy and accomplished printmakers such as Isabel Bishop (1902-1988), Will Barnet (born 1911), Raphael Soyer (1899-1987) and Louis Lozowick (1892-1973). Kipniss quickly became so enamored of printmaking that he purchased a small press and began to pull impressions at home. But as he later recalled of his new enterprise:

> It was magical and thrilling, and it was aggravating:
> I loved the prints and making the plates, but I hated
> the actual printing. After about a year, I gave my press
> to a friend.[5]

4

Fig. 4
Robert Kipniss with Burr Miller at Contemporaries Gallery,
New York, 1977
Photo by Leon Sokolsky

The artist learned from the experience that printing consistent editions was tedious, repetitive, time-consuming labor, and that it required considerable expertise and patience. Further, it gave him a greater appreciation for working collaboratively with a capable, knowledgeable master printer, an appreciation that would only grow as he continued to explore the possibilities of printmaking.

In 1968 Kipniss, anticipating an enthusiastic reception, brought to Roth a selection of the intaglio prints he had created. The dealer, much to his surprise, expressed disappointment. Roth told the artist—for the first time—that he had been expecting him to work in lithography and that he would be a "natural" in the technique. Indeed the dealer, intent on expanding his painter's creative repertoire, had secured unbeknownst to Kipniss a commission for five editions of lithographs. While the artist had worked in a range of intaglio processes at Pratt, he had not tried lithography. But at his trusted dealer's urging, he reluctantly ventured to the Banks Street Atelier. Once again, after overcoming his initial reluctance, Kipniss found himself seduced by a new printmaking technique.

Traditional lithography may be explained in relatively simple terms. An image is drawn with a greasy medium upon a smooth limestone matrix and chemically fixed to the surface with gum arabic and nitric acid. The stone is then dampened and ink is rolled across its surface; the ink clings to the greasy rendering but is repelled by the moistened areas. Next a sheet of paper is placed face down on the matrix, and the image is printed when a bar scrapes across the verso of the sheet as it passes by on the press bed. The resulting impression will indicate the strength of the image, and at this stage the artist can make only minor reductive changes by working into the matrix with a metal point or razor blade. While the foregoing description may sound relatively uncomplicated, in the hands of an unskilled printer lithography can be fraught with complications and problems.

Early on, Kipniss's ambitions in the medium were often frustrated by failures in printing, but fortune soon smiled upon him. The artist was commissioned by Associated American Artists in 1968 to create two lithographs, and its director, Sylvan Cole (1918-2005), sent him to the storied atelier of George C. Miller and Son in New York City. Though the senior Miller had passed away by the time Kipniss began to work in lithography, his son Burr (born 1928) (fig. 4) continued the business of pulling editions for artists.[6] At this studio, the printmaker found a level of accomplished professionalism and aesthetic sensitivity that far surpassed anything he had experienced previously. Thenceforth, for more than two decades he haunted the Miller workshop from each May to August, abandoning his brushes and canvas for limestone matrices and lithograph pencils. The artist recalls the studio as a quiet workplace, usually with only himself, the taciturn Miller and an assistant on hand.

At the Miller studio, the artist limned his images directly on the heavy, bluish limestone surfaces with black, waxy lithograph pencils day after day and conceived of a comfortable and practical method for doing so.

> I learned to stack two by fours on either side of the
> stone and then lay a one-by-six plank across them. This
> way I could place my forearms on the plank suspend-
> ed above the surface of the stone, and, resting my
> weight of my upper body on the plank, I could let my
> right wrist dangle over the edge. If I positioned myself
> in a certain way, I could draw just using the weight of
> the litho pencil.[7]

Using a lithograph pencil razor-sharpened to a keen point, the artist built up images with careful, repeated strokes. Miller, in turn, skillfully printed black and white impressions that faithfully reproduced every subtle mark Kipniss made upon the stone. Where previously he had been excited by the inky blacks of his intaglio impressions, the artist became intrigued with the seemingly infinite range of gray tonalities possible with lithography. After a few years, as demand for his lithographs grew and he was able to afford the greater expense, he began to indulge himself the challenges and rewards of working in color. Initially, the color impressions were taken from specially prepared aluminum or zinc plates and a stone. Kipniss utilized a different plate for each hue, and Miller printed them separately and sequentially onto a sheet, saturating it. The final matrix, or key stone, bearing the densest and most meticulously drawn image, required a heavy black inking to penetrate previously printed hues. But this over-inking sometimes clogged the porous grain of the stone matrix and, despite the master printer's efforts, resulted in printing failures. Eventually, at Miller's urging, Kipniss explored alternative lithography methods to avoid some of the problems encountered with stones. From 1980 to 1987 his images were limned on and printed solely from metal plates and from 1988 to 1990 Mylar films.[8] Though the impressions were suc-cessfully printed, for the artist neither approach was as satisfying either aesthetically or viscerally as printing from stone. By the early 1990s, after the two men had collabo-rated to pull some 450 lithographs, Burr Miller retired. Kipniss continued to print with Miller's sons but after a few years the printmaker, emotionally exhausted by years of difficult printings, abandoned any further pursuit of the technique.

Kipniss's working methods have remained remarkably consistent over the course of his career. Though he will occasionally create an object spontaneously, most prints and paintings are preceded by one or more preparatory drawings. A prolific and gifted draftsman, the artist has accumulated hundreds of these works over the years, ranging from simple, gestural studies to ambitious, fully realized compositions. While some images are derived from direct observation, many more are synthesized from both imagination and life. The drawings are truly the wellspring of all his art, and as he pores through them every few days one or two will "speak" to him and become the subject of his next painting, print, or both. While both a print and canvas often share a single drawing as a source of inspiration, the former is never a mere reproduction of the latter. Every Kipniss impression—like a painting—is conceived of, composed, developed and executed as an independent, original creation. Regardless its source, in every instance he masterfully transforms the image so that the observer may discover what its maker has "seen" in the heat of creativity.

Among the earliest and most ephemeral of Kipniss's landscape prints are the drypoint *Apparations* (cat. no. 1), and a lithograph, *Mountain* (cat. no. 2), both dated 1968. (A drypoint is an intaglio print an artist creates by drawing directly into a metal plate with a sharp needle or similar tool. A burr is produced along edges of the drawn lines and holds the ink, resulting in a velvety line when printed.) In either image, the visual weight rests at the bottom of the sheet; yet a few attenuated saplings reach diagonally into the sky and draw the viewer's attention upward into a broad, cloudless firmament. Both impressions are starkly rendered, airy compositions that glow with a soft, diffuse light. The similarity of these visions reveals their creator's early grasp of such divergent techniques, while their simplified forms remind us that Kipniss has not forgotten the lessons of abstraction. The vantage points the artist has established place the viewer at a considerable remove from his subjects. These, like nearly all of his works, are unpeopled, reflecting not only their creator's reclusive nature but also the solitary experience of creating—or viewing—a work of art.

Closely ensuing impressions reflect the artist's growing assurance with and clear preference for lithography, expanding repertoire of sturdy arboreal forms, and resourceful evocations of light. *Through Trees*, 1971 (cat. no. 8), for example, plays off rigid architectural structures in the lower foreground against dense, agitated leafy forms towering above, the tableau dramatically backlit from beyond the distant ridge. The scene is vigorously drawn on the stone with repeated, heavy, almost expressionist strokes of the pencil. Distinctly visible in the sky are areas where Kipniss has employed a razor blade as a drawing tool, carefully incising massed clusters of line into the stone matrix. Bearing no ink, they leave exposed in the printing the bright white of the paper, creating the illusion of intense light as well as a striking visual texture. In such muscular impressions as *Bare Trees (small)* (cat. no. 4) or *Thick Trees* (cat. no. 7), both dated 1970, broad trunks and stout limbs push literally to the fore. Kipniss has built up their plastic form and suggested their rough bark with precisely placed strokes of his lithograph pencil so that they loom convincingly against the visual foil of flat white skies into the viewer's space. In the dark mass, relatively large scale and powerful vertical thrust of their truncated forms, the trees dominate and dwarf the elements of their environs. These impressions, though strongly representational, have much in common with Robert Conover's (1920-1988) abstract woodcut of 1958, *Collision* (fig. 5). "During the l950s," according to David Acton, this artist created "striking relief prints that capture the energy and spirit of Abstract Expressionism, enhanced by the use of simple means."[9] During much of that decade, Conover—like Kipniss—drew inspiration from nature. *Collision's* jagged, overlapping shapes, heightened by the grain and striations of the woodblock, convincingly suggest space, light, texture and the image of a tree. Moreover, "the top-heavy composition provokes a sense of expectation, for it seems that the image could collapse at any moment."[10] To be certain, the truncated arboreal forms by both artists appear to push mightily against the confining edges of their respective sheets, investing the compositions with a sense of compressed energy. In both, their creators' reverence for nature is evident.

The range of hues the artist introduced into his lithographs of the 1970s and 1980s, which often paralleled those of his canvases, brought a new sensuousness and richness to his prints. At the same time, his compositions—especially the interiors—grew in complexity, sophistication and scale. Both *Interior with Chair and Shadow*, 1976 (cat. no. 12), and *Hillside Place*, 1977 (cat. no. 16),

Fig. 5
Robert Conover (American, 1920-1988)
Collision, 1958
Woodcut, 61.1 x 44.5 cm
Worcester Art Museum, Worcester, Massachusetts. 1998.221

entice the eye into their commodious confines. The rooms are defined by strong light pouring through a window and casting bold shadows across ordinary furniture, various utilitarian vessels or a staircase. Visible through the window is a wooded landscape beneath a pale sky. Both compositions are tranquil dramas of solitude shaped by the artist's skillful manipulation of light, space and shadow, enhanced by a palette of warm earth tones. The subtly erotic *Through Bedroom Curtains*, 1983 (cat. no. 37), on the other hand, alludes to human desire. Therein, Kipniss presents in subdued tones of rose and green a suggestive symphony of repeated verticals; the window frame, the curtains, the cabinet, the post and stiles of the bed rail, as well as the strong diagonal of the phallic tree are revealed through the welcoming aperture. A diffuse light softens the edges and shadows in the room, compacting space and insinuating the physical intimacy of the boudoir. He cleverly combines elements of landscape and interior in yet another direction in the enigmatic *Without, Within*, 1978 (cat. no. 22). A rectilinear structure with tall windows on either side affords the spectator a view through a darkened interior to a flat landscape dominated by a large, leafy tree.

8

Fig. 6
René Magritte (Belgian, 1898-1967)
La condition humaine, 1133
Oil on canvas, 39⅜ x 31⅞ inches
National Gallery of Art: Gift of the Collectors Committee.
1987.55.1
Image ©2004 Board of Trustees, National Gallery of Art,
Washington, D.C.

The shadows of leaves are cast across the structure's exterior wall and window frame. Through the subtle interplay of these shadows and the distant foliage, Kipniss purposefully disrupts for the viewer any quick and simple comprehension of space. Similarly ambiguities are manipulated by Belgian surrealist René Magritte (1898-1967) in his canvas *La condition humaine*, 1933 (fig. 6). In this tableau, when the painter

> placed before a window seen from the inside of a room, a painting representing the very part of the landscape that it hides, (he) introduced confusion between real space and represented space and played on the ambiguity between the two.[11]

Kipniss's contemplative color landscapes were a marked departure from the preceding stark black and white impressions not only in terms of their palette of muted hues but also in content. Throughout these works, vestiges of man are diminished compared to elements of the spacious natural surroundings, especially the myriad trees. For example, the lush verdure in both *Picket Fence II*, 1975 (cat. no. 10) and *To Return*, 1980 (cat. no. 24), despite the rigid, vertical architectural forms that bracket each image and the staccato repeat pattern of the fences in their respective foregrounds, irresistibly draws one's gaze into the distance. The crisply delineated overlapping shapes of natural and man-made forms, thoughtfully structured compositions and carefully modulated color tones and shadows combine to form a deep pictorial space. Bucolic horizontal vistas such as *Secrets*, 1979 (cat. no. 23), *Suspension*, 1982 (cat. no. 31), and *Hillside Illusions*, 1982 (cat. no. 33) appear situated in an indeterminate season of the year and in some generic site conjured from the artist's memory and imagination. Vast, pale skies soar above; below, tall sturdy trees boasting stout limbs and clad with dense foliage are interspersed randomly amongst wiry saplings.

Images such as *Afternoon*, 1976 (cat. no. 14), and *The Entrance*, 1983 (cat. no. 38), position Kipniss in the long tradition of American landscapists and invite comparison to exemplars of the nineteenth-century Hudson River School. For them, the young nation's sprawling, untamed forests and nascent rural settings held the promise of personal freedom and adventure, a well as the potential for wealth and advancement, and were interpreted as signs of the Creator's blessing upon the land and its denizens. Certainly the dean of the Hudson River School disciples, the painter and engraver Asher B. Durand (1796-1886), consistently portrayed this metaphorical relationship between man and nature in America in his tranquil and harmonious compositions. While Kipniss's spacious landscapes are also unmistakably American they do not tempt with material rewards; instead, they offer the metaphysical lure of the fleeting and the intangible, allowing the observer to "grasp that which we can never possess, except for the moment . . ."[12] The trees that populate Durand's images, such as the massive specimen in his *Forenoon*, 1847 (fig. 7), were usually "idealized or composite types distilled out of nature's variety."[13] Emerging from a similar practice is Kipniss's *White Star*, 1982 (cat. no. 34), in which the upraised, leafless limbs of the eponymous anthropomorphic tree seemingly beckon the viewer to enter its realm. Certainly Kipniss would agree with Durand that

Fig. 7
Asher Brown Durand (American, 1796-1886)
Forenoon, 1847
Oil on canvas, 60¼ x 48¼ inches
New Orleans Museum of Art: Gift of the Fine Arts Club of New Orleans. 1916.4

> . . . Trees are like men, differing widely in character; in sheltered spots, or under the influence of culture, they show few contrasting points; peculiarities are pruned . . . away, until there is a general resemblance. But in exposed situations, wild and uncultivated . . . they exhibit striking peculiarities and . . . grand originality.[14]

As previously stated, for more than two decades Kipniss produced impressions of exceptional quality at the Miller studio. While the artist eventually lost interest in pulling lithographs, he was still eager to make prints. By 1990 he decided to return to the mezzotint, an intaglio technique that he had first explored to a limited extent in 1982. The mezzotint, technically simple in comparison to lithography, is a direct reductive process that allows the printmaker to work on the matrices in the comfort of his own studio, and with less dependence upon a master printer's atelier. A special tool known as a rocker is used to roughen a copper plate evenly across its surface. (Kipniss prefers machine-rocked plates for what he deems their greater perfection and, therefore, predictability.) If inked and printed, a ready-to-use mezzotint plate would

10

produce a solid black image. The artist selectively works the surface with a burnisher and scraper to produce areas of subtle or dramatic tonal contrasts in his composition (fig. 8). The more he burnishes an area of the plate, the less ink-holding tooth remains and the lighter the area will print. This process allows the printmaker to achieve an extraordinarily broad range of tones.

Since his return to the mezzotint, Kipniss has been fortunate to retain the services, at various times, of several very capable and perceptive master printers (fig. 9). Indeed, the artist feels that the master printer's role in pulling his mezzotints is even more critical than it was with the lithographs. The mezzotint printer must carefully ink and judiciously wipe the copper plate—keeping the printmaker's aesthetic in mind all the while—before placing a dampened sheet over the matrix and rolling the whole through the press. By repeating this process, the printer may produce as many working proofs as necessary for the printmaker's scrutiny. Upon viewing such an impression, the creator may determine that he needs to work the plate further, or has achieved—or surpassed—his original aesthetic goal. Though Kipniss has printed a few multi-plate color mezzotints and hand colored several others, he has overwhelmingly chosen to explore the rich, infinite range of black and white tones offered by the process.

Kipniss's return to the mezzotint signaled more than a mere change of printmaking techniques; it also ushered in significant alterations in his use of space and compositional structure, as well as a profound change in mood. Indeed, the medium was particularly well-suited to take the printmaker in a darker, more intimate and introspective direction hinted at in the late, stark lithograph entitled *Eaves and Dark Window*, 1989 (cat. no. 49). The progression toward a closer physical and emotional engagement with his subjects is manifested in such impressions as *Sentinels*, 1992 (cat. no. 51), *Houses & sheds*, 1999 (cat. no. 68), and *Clear vase & landscape*, 1995 (cat. no. 55), which reflect Kipniss's placing of his subjects closer to the picture plane. In the first two he establishes a vantage point nearer the

Fig. 10
George Inness
(American, 1825-1894)
The Home of the Heron,
1893
Oil on canvas,
30 x 45 inches
The Art Institute of
Chicago: Edward B.
Butler Collection.
1911.31
Photograph by Greg
Williams.Photography
©The Art Institute of
Chicago

huddled trees and buildings. Then, with dramatic treatment of light and shadow, he delineates their distinct shapes and volumes and draws our gaze toward a slice of sky visible above the elevated horizon line. The visual elements of *Clear vase and landscape* constitute a hypnotic visual experience that compresses space even more. The transparent vessel that dominates the center foreground rests directly upon the bottom edge of the image, and the leafy arrangement within it draws the eye skyward. The dense arboreal forms that dot the landscape beyond promenade from a hazy distance through flashes of light and shadow and through the lens of the vase. *Sentinels II*, 1998 (cat. no. 64), exudes an even greater sense of mystery and, in the artist's words, "haunting intensity," than the previous images. Therein, from the middle distance beyond a trio of sinewy, attenuated limbs, a luxuriant tree slowly emerges like a specter from the crepuscular gloom. Only the few fluttering leaves in the darkness at the bottom left and the eerie glow at the top of the sheet are clues that our gaze is oriented not toward the earth, but upward into the trees and heavens beyond.

The foregoing mezzotints powerfully echo certain aspects of the paintings of George Inness (1825-1894). Unlike many of his American contemporaries, he was influenced by French Barbizon practitioners such as Camille-Jean-Baptiste Corot (1796-1875) and Charles-François Daubigny (1817-1878), for whom nature offered both a virtual and spiritual escape from the rapid urbanization and industrialization of their day. Inness, certainly one of the most "modern" American painters of the late nineteenth century, was in his canvases of 1884 to 1894 more interested in solving formalist problems of landscape composition than faithfully imitating nature. The otherwordly *The Home of the Heron*, 1893 (fig. 10), like this master's other works of the period, was inspired by an actual physical location. Kipniss's landscapes, in contrast,

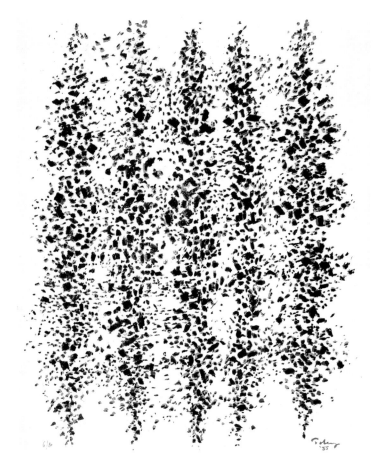

emanate not so much from direct retinal experience as from the mind's eye. Like his predecessor, however, he is vitally concerned with the spiritual in art and undoubtedly would agree with Inness's notion that the primary purpose of a work of art is "but to awaken an emotion."[15] Moreover, a feature found in the works of both practitioners

. . . is their atmospheric effect, in which all things are enveloped by a thick mist; their heavy, dense atmosphere does not resemble the visible characteristics of nature, but is an invention—an artificial artistic device for necessity of pictorial unity. Furthermore, . . . (their) . . . compositional organization . . . is extremely beautiful in abstract terms.[16]

Elements of Kipniss's visual inventiveness and personal beliefs that surface in his ensuing semiabstract prints are echoed in certain works by Mark Tobey (1890-1976), whose paintings exerted considerable influence upon the New York School practitioners. Tobey is best recognized for his signature, abstract calligraphic style, which he termed "white writing." A deeply spiritual creator influenced by his Baha'i faith, study of Zen Buddhism and music, he attributed his creative impulses, in great measure, to the result of lifelong meditation. The observation that "Tobey's art . . . is an analogy for the unifying principles of the natural universe and the spiritual energy that unites humanity to the cosmos"[17] reverberates in Kipniss's statement that in his work he is "communicating something essential to all humanity, something essential to the human experience."[18]
In Tobey's color lithograph of 1955, entitled *Composition* (fig. 11),

tiny brushstrokes cluster like iron filings to bar magnets, delineating unseen fields of force . . . it is as if he has painted the interstices between the lines, allowing the colored paper to create his white writing. The varied size of the . . . daubs, their subtle tones, and seemingly random placement are . . . reminiscent of light.[19]

Fig. 12
Robert Goodnough
(American, born 1917)
Untitled, 1976
Color screenprint,
48 x 58 inches
New Orleans Museum
of Art: Gift of Mrs. John
Weinstock. 19 94.176

Much of the foregoing description also suggests the nature of the delicious ambiguities to be found in Kipniss's *For Stella*, 1998 (cat. no. 65), *The white forest*, 2000 (cat. no. 75), and *Tall trees at night*, 2001 (cat. no. 77). (Indeed, the artist has reminded the author that the myriad leaves in *For Stella* were created by his painstakingly burnishing the space *around* each of them). In these images the audience is no longer placed at a distance from the scene but instead is now surrounded by it. Masterfully employing a range of tones, he carefully compacts space and adroitly manipulates the overall surface pattern created by pulsating patches of light, shadow, trunk and foliage, essentially "camouflaging" his image. The beholder is rewarded with full recognition of the scene only after he patiently allows his eyes to adjust, as they would in a dense forest, to the dark. As he draws ever closer to his subject, Kipniss's landscapes grow increasingly abstract. This is reflected in the elegant, umbrous and spectral visions *Forest Nocturne III*, 2000 (cat. no. 72), *Incandescence*, 2000 (cat. no. 73), and *Illuminata*, 2001 (cat. no. 80), which are decidedly minimalist and evince a certain sparing musicality. Each impression presents a copse of slender, bare trees with intertwining branches, all set against a solid black background. Unevenly illuminated from an equivocal source, they appear to advance and recede alternately in space; the trees and branches, along with the inky interstices between them and the edges of the plate, establish a carefully orchestrated rhythm.

Window w/bench & trees, 1999 (cat. no. 70), *Garden shadows*, 2000 (cat. no. 71), and *Window w/vase & forest*, 2000 (cat. no. 74), not only continue the sense of musicality but also reexamine the window motif. The foreground of *Garden shadows* is dominated by a register of stout, white trunks adorned with a thick

14

canopy of small, dark leaves. These luminous verticals, set against thin, dark saplings visible in the background, establish a horizontal, syncopated rhythm. The procession of arboreal forms is surrounded by a black, inner compositional frame, or "window," that effectively isolates, suspends in space, and places it at an indeterminate distance from the viewer. (The overall effect is not only suggestive of a view from a darkened room through an aperture; it is also uncannily reminiscent of a cinematic illusion flickering on the screen in a theater.) In the foregrounds of *Window w/bench & trees* and *Window w/vase & forest*, Kipniss places large, sinuous leaves on diagonal branches. Illuminated from behind, their botanical shapes stand in bold contrast to the dark rectilinear elements of the interiors. As their scale grows, so does the importance of shape in these synthesized leaves, whose serpentine contours evoke sensuous, melodic movement. Through this efficacious juxtaposition, these leafy "ladders" lead the eye up and through the composition.

The abstract essence of the leaf forms in Kipniss's aforementioned representational images are strongly echoed in the clustered organic shapes—what Clement Greenberg termed "facet-leaves"—of an untitled color screenprint of 1976 (fig. 12) by second-generation Abstract Expressionist Robert Goodnough (American, born 1917). This sheet, with its lilting musicality and spatial play of richly hued fragments undulating before a screen of pale vertical striations, strongly echoes the two *Window* images. Goodnough's description of the correlation between music and his "facet-leaves" recalls Kipniss's leaves:

> To me, the shapes are something like musical notes. It's almost as if the . . . shapes were sounds. They appeal to you in the same sense the musical sounds do. You don't relate the sounds to something you've heard before, and in the same way, the shapes in my paintings should not be related to anything outside of themselves. They are just part of a composition . . . . It's the same as a musical composition; so it does relate to music.[20]

The Kipniss impressions from the extensive James F. White collection offer valuable insights into the artist's creative odyssey as a printmaker. Ranging from his earliest efforts to his most recent, this body of work reveals his ever-expanding technical mastery of printmaking, continually evolving aesthetic sensibility and considered content. The comparisons of this creator's images with those of other significant artists illuminate not only intriguing parallels but also critical differences that place the artist in his own niche. In his relentless pursuit of aesthetic perfection and imagery *sui generis*, this creator has continued to push his personal boundaries ever further. Certainly Kipniss's remarkable accomplishments as a printmaker serve to remind the viewer that, as Rainer Maria Rilke opined in his *Letters*,

Works of art are indeed always products of having-been-in-danger, of having-gone-to-the-very-end in an experience, to where man can go no further.

DANIEL PIERSOL
Deputy Director of Programs
Mississippi Museum of Art

NOTES:

1. Though his mother often accompanied him to the theater, Kipniss also recalls going to see films by himself as young as seven years of age. Lhomme's knowledge of European cinema certainly whetted Kipniss's appetite for more. The two instituted a film club at the college, subsidized by the student council, and rented foreign films from the Museum of Modern Art in New York for nonprofit showings. Now a distinguished cinematographer, Lhomme has participated in the making of such films as *Camille Claudel*, *Les Palmes de Monsieur Schutz*, *Cyrano de Bergerac* and *Jefferson in Paris*.
2. Robert Hughes, *Goya* (New York: Alfred A. Knopf, 2003), 175.
3. Lawrence Campbell, *Art News*, October 1953, 56.
4. Robert Kipniss, "Lithography: A Review of My Experience," *Robert Kipniss: Lithographs from the Artist's Archives, 1968-1990* (San Francisco: Weinstein Gallery, 2002), 2.
5. Ibid.
6. Established in 1917, George Miller's (1894-1965) was the first American studio committed to the production of artists' prints. The impressions he pulled as master printer in collaboration with George Bellows (1882-1925) and later, Grant Wood (1892-1942), Thomas Hart Benton (1889-1975) and Rockwell Kent (1882-1971), helped to establish lithography as a fine art printmaking technique in this country. Burr apprenticed with his father.
7. Robert Kipniss, "Lithography: A Review of My Experience," *Robert Kipniss: Lithographs from the Artist's Archives, 1968-1990* (San Francisco: Weinstein Gallery, 2002), 5.
8. These are offset prints, created when the lithographic image is mechanically transferred from the plate to a rubber cylinder, then onto an adjacent cylinder and printed. The compositions on Mylar were first "burned" onto a light-sensitive aluminum plate, then printed.
9. David Acton, *The Stamp of Impulse: Abstract Expressionist Prints* (Worcester, Massachusetts, Worcester Art Museum, 2001), 156.

10. Ibid.

11. Gise'le Ollinger-Zinque, "The Cultivation of Ideas: 'The Invisible Cannot Be Hidden from our Eyes'," *René Magritte, 1898-1967* (Belgium: Brussels Royal Museums of Fine Arts of Belgium, 1998), 22.

12. Telephone interview with the artist, February 2, 2005.

13. *The Dictionary of Art* (Groves's Dictionaries Inc., New York, 1996) edited by Jane Turner, 419.

14. Patricia Anderson, "The Savage State," *The Course of the Empire: The Erie Canal and the New York Landscape, 1825-1875* (New York: Memorial Art Gallery of the University of Rochester, 1984), 22.

15. George W. Neubert, "George Inness: His Signature Years and the Modernist Tradition," *George Inness: His Signature Years 1884-1894* (Oakland: The Oakland Museum Art, 1978), *7*.

16. Ibid., 8

17. Acton, *The Stamp of Impulse: Abstract Impressionist Prints* (Worcester, Mass.: Worchester Art Museum, 2001), 134.

18. Telephone interview with the artist, February 2, 2005.

19. Acton, *The Stamp of Impulse: Abstract Impressionist Prints* (Worcester, Mass.: Worchester Art Museum, 2001), 134.

20. Martin H. Bush, "Talking with Robert Goodnough," *Goodnough* (New York: Abbeville Press, 1982), 235-36.

SOLILOQUY
KIPNISS ON KIPNISS

To keep me occupied, my mother sometimes would say, "I want you to sit here and do some drawing." I was three or four years old. She'd say, "draw me a plane," and I'd draw an airplane, she'd say "draw me a car," so I'd draw a car. One day she said, "draw me a typewriter," and I drew a typewriter. She looked at me and asked, "where did you ever see a typewriter?" because we didn't have one. It amused her, it amused my father a little bit and they were pleased that I had this skill. As I progressed through school it didn't seem like such a big deal. But then there came a point in college where I really got very interested in painting, and I decided to pursue it. I was a junior in the English department at Iowa, and working in the painting studio. I painted up a storm. A delegation of graduate students came around after about four months, and I had about one hundred paintings. They said, "Kipniss, what are you going to do with all of these paintings?" I said, "I'm going to have a one man show in New York." They looked at me like I was a lunatic. I felt like a nut for having said what I said, so I went to the art library and looked at books and magazines for the names of galleries. I was thinking I would take a few paintings east with me at Easter break to see if I could scare something up at one of the galleries in New York. There was a gallery at 57th Street advertising a competition for a one-man show, so I entered. I came in second but they liked my work so much they decided to give me the one-man show as well. So I had a one-man show in New York, although my parents didn't know why. They presumed I would go on to a career in teaching and that I would paint on weekends. Two years later I had a second one-man show; they saw I was going to pursue it and just went bananas.

I hardly ever saw my father after that for many, many years. The more shows I had, the more distressed and envious he got. At one show he looked around and said, "You can't sign your name Kipniss." I said, "Why not?" and he said "Because that's *my* name." My mother shared very much his feelings until I started to exhibit, get my name in the papers and make some money. Then she was so proud to see the family name in the paper and, of course, all the other members of the family who hadn't spoken to me for ages started coming to the openings and having their pictures taken with me.

I can't say that I'm against learning or being taught but when it comes to art, my feeling is that you cannot separate form from content. As soon as someone starts teaching you form, style, and technique, they are teaching you themselves, too, and there is something impure going on. You are not going to be able to get to the heart of what you are trying to express and you will learn someone else's technique, but can you go beyond that? I did not want to have what I needed to do polluted, tainted, influenced by someone else's shortcomings. Frankly, if Picasso himself wanted to teach me, I don't think I would have wanted to study with him because I didn't want to be a little Picasso. I wanted to fail or succeed strictly on my own terms. If you want to find that uniqueness in your work , you have to invent a way of expressing it; you have to find out how to do it. You invent how to do it.

I knew very early on that no burst of energy would produce a good amount of really significant work, that if you want to accomplish anything—and this was my mantra from the time I was seventeen or eighteen years old—do a full day's work every day. The shape of your career will take care of itself if you do a good day's work every day, be self-critical, be self-analytical and learn from what you are doing. If the work is there, everything else will follow. I noticed as a student that whatever was hot in the newspapers or magazines you would see on the easels in the studio and a few months later, something else was hot and they'd all be doing that. These people were clearly out of touch with themselves. I felt from a very early age that if you try and understand what the critics and public are looking for you fail, and you will never understand what you were capable of. You might as well fail for what you really are as to fail for what you are not.

I began as an abstract painter. I thought, well that's great, you can accomplish and express everything you want and really get to the heart of it. After about a year or two, I didn't think I was really getting to the heart of anything. I needed imagery. I didn't have a sense of limitation, so I did figure painting. Then I did a still life, then a landscape. But I'd get something nice through landscapes, a kind of magic that I wasn't achieving in the figure paintings. I thought that if I could paint really good land-scapes, maybe I could really get somewhere with it. But the more I went into imagery the more alienated I became from what was going on then in New York, and the more puzzled the art dealers were when they saw my work. They would say, that's not for us. I just continued doing what I was doing.

Panoramas almost don't exist in my work anymore. I'm really not interested in them but I am interested in closer space, in relationships and different spaces rather than one larger view. I think that in general I have gone closer into my subject, mostly to get a better abstraction of it. I'm really looking at an interesting choice of words. I know there's no question that as I get older, my work becomes more abstract. I'm intrigued by the ambiguity of seeing the abstraction as an abstraction and as an object, and one that's readable.

When I was five, we moved to a little town in Long Island called Laurelton. It was quite rural at that time. Houses were on small lots, but there was a lot of undeveloped land. There were woods nearby and, frankly, I was quite miserable at home. My only relief was to go into the woods and play. I had friends and I played with them, too, but my greatest pleasure was going into the woods alone. I was going to a different reality. It was real; it wasn't escape. I mean, to escape you watch an escapist movie, read an escapist novel and you're taken out of your life. I was going to a deeper part of my own psyche, my own life, my own experience. I would go into the woods and look at the trees, listen to the breeze and see the leaves moving. I'd walk around with an imaginary friend and come home feeling nurtured and revitalized. As an artist, I can't get over the feeling I have when I am alone in the woods, doing my landscapes. It has comforted me since I was five years old and has been a wonderful experience for me. When I'm in those places, I find a deeper part of myself that brings me peace.

I have always felt that wherever you are, everything is there. You just have to learn how to see it. While I have worked with a limited number of subjects—trees, houses, chairs—it's really very limitless. I know this by having gone back to the same landscape over a period of time; every time I go there, I see a different landscape. I have gone back, for instance, many times to Springfield, Ohio, where I went to school for two years. I used to walk those alleys, and I just loved the intimacy of walking through the trenches of people's lives in those suburban alleys. They had no driveways between the houses, and the blocks were bisected by alleys where people drove to put up their cars. Small sheds, garages and little structures would be thirty, forty, fifty feet from the main houses, with gables rising up above. I'd walk through and maybe it would be starting to get dark, and here is someone rattling pots and pans, there blaring a radio, or a kid crying. It was fascinating. Not just visually, but aurally, too. I started going back there around 1979, and have returned ten to twelve or more times to go on sketching trips. Whenever I go back, I don't see the same place. Of course, what I'm looking for is the place I knew when I was seventeen. Nothing's changed physically, thank goodness, it's all intact. But I don't have seventeen-year-old eyes anymore. Things looked different then, I've got a lot of mileage. It's fascinating to see what I'm so familiar with, but with more understanding and more nuance. I have become so familiar with things, but they're *not* familiar. They're new because you keep looking, you keep your eyes open. The more familiar I become with them, the stranger these things become.

In my pictures the viewer becomes *me*, and what you don't realize is that *I'm* becoming the objects in the image. I pose for my trees. I catch myself, as I'm drawing a tree, in the posture of the tree. If it's going off to the right, I'm like this, if it's going off to the left, I'm like that, so I'm assuming the posture of the tree. I don't try to create an objective vantage point. It's very definitely my eyes, up-close into this image. It's as though I could swoop down and put your face right in there, and you're alone in this place, with this vision, this atmosphere. If someone looks at my paintings and sees only trees and houses, then they don't see what I'm doing. I may be painting trees and houses, but when I look at them, that's not what I see. I see an atmosphere, a moment, a quickly passing experience that I'm trying to capture. My art is an art of intensity, of delving, of exploring the soul.

I painted and wrote until I was thirty. After that, a lot of the poetry went into the art. There's always the subtext of eternity, this sense of mortality that distresses me and yet makes life so beautiful, so precious. I want my titles to open a viewer up to experience the painting, so I choose them with great care. I like them to be descriptive in a way, such as *Reminiscences* or *Incandescence*, because those words have some meaning and yet it's not limited. It's more open than closed.

I don't know why I didn't want to make prints except it just seemed so labor intensive, and I wasn't too sure what you ended up with. I hadn't seen a lot of great prints. I had only seen student prints, and I had never really investigated what prints were. I didn't see the point in making multiples if people weren't interested in uniques. In other words, if I made paintings and drawings, and I wasn't selling those, why would I want to make an image and print twenty, thirty, forty of them and then have twenty, thirty, forty of something not to sell? I wanted to study other subjects but when it came to art, I didn't want to *study* it, I wanted to *do* it and I was *eager* to do it, bursting with energy. But the other problem was the head of that department at Iowa—it was a one-person print department really—a guy Mauricio Lasansky. He was very autocratic, he really ran a tight ship, and I wasn't interested in being a sailor on a tight ship. So I didn't see the point until around 1967. Murray Roth, who ran the FAR Gallery in New York, was a very enthusiastic supporter of my work. He insisted I make prints, even though I didn't want to. I finally went and took a course in printmaking, fully intending to drop out after the first night. It was a six-week course, three evenings a week. But the teacher, Robert de Lamonicio, was fabulous, he was lucid, he was logical, he was human. I took notes, I listened to what he had to say, and he explained the process of printmaking.

I made some nice prints and I brought them to FAR Gallery. Roth said "No, no, no, no, not etchings—lithographs! You were born to make lithographs. You have to make lithographs." I said, "I don't know anything about lithography, and I don't want to go to school anymore." Then Murray said, "I got you a commission for five lithographs! Go down to the Bank Street Atelier, you'll watch for twenty minutes and you'll pick it up and you'll make a lithograph. It's no trick, not hard, they'll print it, you just have to draw on the stone." I went down there. It didn't take twenty minutes. I was very comfortable with it, and I started drawing on a stone. I made some nice prints and I got hooked. Loved the texture of drawing on a stone; that was sexual, the feeling of drawing on the stone, and then seeing these multiples beautifully printed. One thing led to another, and I got into the George C. Miller workshop. Burr Miller printed for me, and I was selling now so I could afford the paper.

Burr was a marvelous printer, always looking for the right way to do things. He did things old school—oh yeah, very old school—which I liked anyway. I liked making prints as long as someone else was printing. When I started making prints, I started *looking* at prints and then I realized there were a lot of great, beautiful things made in print. It's a whole astounding world, a universe. It seemed very worthwhile to make prints when I realized that there was such a world to explore, but when I was in school I wasn't aware of what could be done with the print. I hadn't looked at prints, didn't know what great prints were. It had never occurred to me.

I used to spend four months a year at the Miller studio. I would begin in May and work through August. They would get there at seven, I'd get in around 7:30 and would work on stones in one corner where Burr set me up. Burr would leave at 4:00, his helper would leave around 5:30, and I would stay until he closed up. So I was there every day from 7:30 until 5:30, five days a week for four months. I did that from 1968 to 1990, twenty-two , twenty-three years. If I finished a stone, they'd print a proof of it. I would get a proof of all my black and whites; and. then when I finished all these, I would do the color separations. Burr would print the color sheets, and then they had to print the black key stones over them. Then I would spend two weeks doing color proofing of all the prints I had done that year. I would leave with six good prints, and they would have one proof of each. A couple of weeks later I'd get delivery of all these prints, and sign them.

The nature of mezzotint is that it is about objects emerging from darkness, catching light and being defined by their shadows as well as by their highlights. If you wanted to do something lighter or airier, you would use a drypoint or a lithograph. That's what happens in mezzotint and is why I really fell so much in love with it. It enables me to achieve the density that frequently eluded me in lithography.

It takes tremendous focus, but the sensitivity of an intaglio printer is really important. For example, a copper plate print, such as a mezzotint, must be wiped by hand with special care. Most prints have a passage that poses some problem where he has to wipe it a little more or wipe it a little less, and give it a little "something." I could say to him, I like what's happening here, but I would like this area darker, and he could leave a little more ink there. An intaglio printer has to have an instinct for which ink or paper will better bring out a particular image, and he can use more pressure in the press, which can alter the image dramatically. In lithography you can't do that. You roll (ink) up the stone, and that's what you get. Or if it's going through the offset press, printing on a metal plate, whatever you drew is what's going to print. He can't make half of it a little darker or get it a little lighter in this area.

I do not start a print with a finished drawing all the time. Many times I start with just a little sketch, or sometimes I'll even have a painting in mind. The most important thing for me to have plotted out before I start working on a plate is the composition. The proportions are crucial because one of the things that makes it work is that very delicate interrelationship of all the shapes. I have tried to do things on a not-quite-the-right-proportion plate, or not-quite-the-right proportion canvas. But you can't take a composition that's basically ten by 12 inches and put it into a format that is really ten by nine inches or ten by 13 inches because it isn't going to look right. It may become something else, and it may become something else that's very good, but it's not going to be what you had set out after. So, what I am basically looking for in a drawing is proportion, a certain kind of graphic magic, and then I will take that and draw the bare outlines of different objects in pencil lightly on the plate. Then I'll start working. Hopefully it will work but I have to extemporize all the shading and detail. If I draw a tree, I'll draw a trunk and maybe some major branches, but the exact curve will emerge when it gets larger. You've got to be inventive.

The most ambitious print I have ever completed is *For Stella*, which is composed of thousands of leaves. Of course, when you do a mezzotint, you don't draw the leaves, you draw the space *around* each leaf. I had the trunks drawn in first, then began on the foliage. Starting in the top right hand corner, I would extemporize leaves in a three- by four-inch area one day, and the next I would come in and do an adjacent three- by four-inch space. The next working session I had to integrate those two areas. I repeated this process until I had gone across the entire top four inches of the plate. Then directly below this register I began again from one edge, burnishing my way across and down and every time I did a three- by four-inch area. Of course, I also had to integrate all these individual areas. Now this is a twenty- by twenty-inch plate. I'm not sure what everybody's definition of the term "zen" is, but I'd guess we would all say that it is some sort of internalized, meditative sort of spiritual state where you focus on a particular image or a particular thought. Very trance-like, I suppose. I do know when I was doing those leaves I would get into a zone, and it was very pleasurable. I used to go to sleep dreaming about copper leaves, and often I had dreams about them. In order to make leaves, you *didn't do* the leaves—that's the most zen thing I could possibly think of.

When I was twenty years old I said to myself, "I don't want to be an old man of forty-five and wonder what I might have accomplished if I had tried hard." Now I'm seventy-four, but I don't have any second thoughts about what I might have done if I had tried harder because I did the best I could every day. You need to have a hunger to do this, because nobody *wants* you to be an artist, no one *needs* you to be artist, no one is *waiting* for your art. If you do something wonderful, they will find you indispensable, but no one knows if you are going to do that or not. Least of all the artist himself.

Excerpted from an interview with the artist
conducted by Daniel Piersol on March 9, 2005.

SELECTED WORKS

1. *Apparitions*, 1968, drypoint, 11⅝ x 9⅞
signed *Kipniss* and *20/30*
printed by the artist

225/250   mountains   Kipniss

2. *Mountain*, 1968, lithograph, 11⅞ x 8⅞
signed *Kipniss* and *225/250*

3. *Sheds and Fence*, 1969, lithograph, 12 x 18
signed *Kipniss* and *41/90*

4. *Bare Trees (small)*, 1970, lithograph, 13⅞ x 10
signed *Kipniss* and *12/90*

7. *Thick Trees*, 1970, lithograph, 11⅞ x 15⅞
signed *Kipniss* and *printer's proof*
edition 90

8. *Through Trees*, 1971, lithograph, 13 ⅞ x 9 ⅞
signed *Kipniss* and *7/15*

10. *Picket Fence II,* 1975, color lithograph, 18 x 13 ½
signed *Kipniss* and *artist's proof, xiv/xxv*
edition 150

33

11. *Interior with Suspended Plant*, 1975, color lithograph, 23⅞ x 17⅞
signed *Kipniss* and *5/90*

12. *Interior with Chair and Shadow*, 1976, color lithograph, 24 x 17¾
signed *Kipniss* and *8/90*

13. *Reflections*, 1976, color lithograph, 20 x 15
signed *Kipniss* and *62/90*

7/90   Kipniss

14. *Afternoon*, 1976, color lithograph, 19⅞ x 15⅞
signed *Kipniss* and *7/90*

37

15. *Winter*, 1977, color lithograph, 17 x 12⅞
signed *Kipniss* and *xv/xx*
edition 100

16. *Hillside Place*, 1977, color lithograph, 19⅝ x 14⅜
signed *Kipniss* and *artist's proof, xv/xxv*

5/120   *Green Roofs*   Kipniss

19. *Green Roofs*, 1978, color lithograph, 16 ⅜ x 14 ¾
signed *Kipniss* and *5/120*

5/120   Shadows II   Kipniss

20. *Shadows II*, 1978, color lithograph, 16⅝ x 15¾
signed *Kipniss* and *5/120*

21. *Gateway*, 1978, color lithograph, 13⅞ x 13⅞
signed *Kipniss* and *artist's proof, viii/xxv*
edition 150

22. *Without, Within*, 1978, color lithograph, 24 x 18
signed *Kipniss* and *4/120*

23. *Secrets*, 1979, color lithograph, 15⅞ x 19⅞
signed *Kipniss* and *8/120*

24. *To Return*, 1980, color lithograph, 23½ × 18
signed *Kipniss* and *7/120*

25. *Reminiscences*, 1980, color lithograph, 23½ × 18
signed *Kipniss* and *artist's proof, viii/xxv*
edition 175

46

26. *Spring Secrets*, 1980, color lithograph, 19 x 24
signed *Kipniss* and *11/120*

27. *Window with Leaves*, 1980, color lithograph, 16 x 14
signed *Kipniss* and *11/120*

28. *Ohio Night,* 1981, color lithograph, 16¾ x 16
signed *Kipniss* and *9/120*

artist's proof xx/xxv   Kipniss

29. *Interlude*, 1981, color lithograph, 13 x 14
signed *Kipniss* and *artist's proof, xx/xxv*
edition 275

31. *Suspension*, 1982, color lithograph, 18 x 22
signed *Kipniss* and *28/120*

33. *Hillside Illusions*, 1982, color lithograph, 15 x 15½
signed *Kipniss* and *artist's proof, xix/xxx*
edition 250

52

34. *White Star*, 1982, color lithograph, 15 x 13
signed *Kipniss* and *28/120*

33/150   Kipniss

35. *Souvenirs,* 1982, color lithograph, 13 ½ x 10
signed *Kipniss* and *33/150*

36. *Studio Flowers*, 1982, color lithograph, 24 x 18
signed *Kipniss* and *28/120*

37. *Through Bedroom Curtains*, 1983, color lithograph, 20 x 18
signed *Kipniss* and *13/120*

38. *The Entrance*, 1983, color lithograph, 22 x 18
signed *Kipniss* and *13/120*

39. *A Private Porch*, 1984, color lithograph, 17 x 16
signed *Kipniss* and *2/120*

41. *Just Before the Sun*, 1985, color lithograph, 12 x 11
signed *Kipniss* and *6/120*

59

44. *Window with Orange Curtain*, 1987, color lithograph, 17 ½ x 14
signed *Kipniss* and *40/120*

artist's proof   *Streets & alleys, afternoon*   Kipniss

45. *Streets and Alleys, Afternoon,* 1987, color lithograph, 11 x 12¾
signed *Kipniss* and *artist's proof*
edition 120

61

47. *The Blue Stove*, 987, color lithograph, 17½ x 14
signed *Kipniss* and *2/120*

49. *Eaves and Dark Windows*, 1989, color lithograph, 14 x 14
signed *Kipniss* and *6/120*

51. *Sentinels*, 1992, mezzotint, 13⅞ x 9
signed *Kipniss* and *artist's proof, ii/x*

trial proof   Springfield, O. for James White, in friendship, 8.7.02   Kipniss

53. *Springfield, O.*, 1992, drypoint, 12 x 10⅞
signed *Kipniss, trial proof* and *for James White, in friendship, 8.7.02*

15/60   Kipniss

54. *Backyards, evening,* 1995, mezzotint, 9⅜ x 7
signed *Kipniss* and *15/60*

55. *Clear vase & landscape*, 1995, mezzotint, 9 ⅜ x 14
signed *Kipniss* and 66/75

56. *To the reservoir*, 1995, mezzotint, 9⅝ x 7
signed *Kipniss* and *21/40*

58. *Alleys, Springfield,* 1995, mezzotint, 7 x 7⅞
signed *Kipniss* and *artist's proof, viii/x*

60. *August night*, 1996, mezzotint, 7 ⅞ x 7
signed *Kipniss* and 9/60

70

61. *Easel & trees w/ moon,* 1996, mezzotint, 14 x 9⅝
signed *Kipniss* and *22/60*

62. *Hillside shadows*, 1997, mezzotint, 11⅝ x 9⅜
signed *Kipniss* and *artist's proof*

63. *Still life w/spoon*, 1998, mezzotint, 9⅝ x 11⅝
signed *Kipniss* and 3/50

64. *Sentinels II* (first state), 1998, mezzotint, 14 x 9 ⅜
signed *Kipniss* and *14/50*

74

65. *For Stella*, 1998, mezzotint, 19 x 19
signed *Kipniss* and *artist's proof*

66. *Still life w/kettle & cup,* 1998, mezzotint, 14 x 9 ⅝
signed *Kipniss* and *14/50*

68. *Houses & sheds,* 1999, mezzotint, 11⅜ x 9⅜
signed *Kipniss* and *38/50*

69. *Vase w/small branches,* 1999, mezzotint, 9⅜ x 6
signed *Kipniss* and *b.a.t.*

70. *Window w/bench & trees*, 1999, 19⅞ x 15⅜
signed *Kipniss* and *39/60*

71. *Garden shadows,* 2000, mezzotint, 11⅞ x 9⅜
signed *Kipniss* and *20/60*

72. *Forest nocturne III*, 2000, mezzotint, 14 x 9 ¾
signed *Kipniss* and *trial proof*

9/60

Kipniss

73. *Incandescence,* 2000, mezzotint, 7⅞ x 7
signed *Kipniss* and 9/60

74. *Window w/vase & forest*, 2000, mezzotint, 19½ x 19½
signed *Kipniss* and *38/60*
Collection of New Orleans Museum of Art; Gift of James F. White
in honor of his parents, Agnes and Richard White, 2002.217

83

75. *The white forest,* 2000, mezzotint, 23⅞ x 17
signed *Kipniss* and *20/60*
Collection of New Orleans Museum of Art: Gift of James F. White
in honor of his parents, Agnes and Richard White, 2002.221

76. *Crossings*, 2001, mezzotint, 11⅜ x 9⅜
signed *Kipniss* and *9/60*
Collection of New Orleans Museum of Art: Gift of James F. White
in honor of his parents, Agnes and Richard White, 2002.219

77. *Tall trees at night,* 2001, mezzotint, 19⅝ x 13
signed *Kipniss* and *34/60*
Collection of New Orleans Museum of Art: Gift of James F. White
in honor of his parents, Agnes and Richard White, 2002.218

78. *Forest nocturne IV*, 2001, mezzotint, 19⅞ x 14
signed *Kipniss* and *artist's proof, vi/x*
Collection of New Orleans Museum of Art: Gift of James F. White
in honor of his parents, Agnes and Richard White, 2002.220

trial proof   Kipniss

79. *Still life w/dark window*, 2001, mezzotint, 14 x 9⅞
signed *Kipniss* and *trial proof*

artists proof xvi/xx   Kipniss

80. *Illuminata*, 2001, mezzotint, 7 ⅞ x 7
signed *Kipniss* and *artist's proof, xvi/xx*

12/60   Kipniss

82. *Still life w/chair & standing lamp,* 2002, mezzotint, 11⅝ x 9⅜
signed *Kipniss* and *12/60*

artist's proof I/XII   Kipniss

83. *Interior w/cup, spoon & window, 2003, mezzotint, 7 x 5*
signed Kipniss and artist's proof, i/xii

84. *Two vases*, 2004, mezzotint, 19½ x 15⅝
signed *Kipniss* and *artist's proof*, *ix/xiii*

85. *The balanced rock*, 2004, mezzotint, 19½ x 19⅜
signed *Kipniss* and *artist's proof*, iv/xv

86. *Nocturne: still life w/two vases*, 2004, mezzotint, 19½ x 13
signed *Kipniss* and *74/75*

CATALOGUE OF THE EXHIBITION

All selections lent by the James F. White Collection, unless otherwise noted. Works are measured in inches, height before width and record image size. All lithographs printed at George C. Miller and Son, New York City. Mezzotint printers: Bruce Cleveland, 1990-1992; Kathy Caraccio, 1995-2002; Anthony Kirk at Center for Contemporary Printmaking, Norwalk, Connecticut, 2003-present. *Asterisk indicates entries is not illustrated.

1. *Apparitions*, 1968, drypoint, 11⅝ x 9⅞
signed *Kipniss* and *20/30*
printed by the artist

2. *Mountain*, 1968, lithograph, 11⅞ x 8⅞
signed *Kipniss* and *225/250*

3. *Sheds and Fence*, 1969, lithograph, 12 x 18
signed *Kipniss* and *41/90*

4. *Bare Trees (small)*, 1970, lithograph, 13⅞ x 10
signed *Kipniss* and *12/90*

***5.** *Backyard I*, 1970, lithograph, 15¾ x 16¾
signed *Kipniss* and *60/75*

***6.** *Still Life with Bottle*, 1970, lithograph, 10 x 15⅞
signed *Kipniss* and *8/90*

7. *Thick Trees*, 1970, lithograph, 11⅞ x 15⅞
signed *Kipniss* and *printer's proof*
edition 90

8. *Through Trees*, 1971, lithograph, 13⅞ x 9⅞
signed *Kipniss* and *7/15*

9. *Bush*, 1971, lithograph, 13½ x 10
signed *Kipniss* and *artist's proof for printer*
edition 260

10. *Picket Fence II*, 1975, color lithograph, 18 x 13½
signed *Kipniss* and *artist's proof, xiv/xxv*
edition 150

11. *Interior with Suspended Plant*, 1975, color lithograph,
23⅞ x 17⅞
signed *Kipniss* and *5/90*

12. *Interior with Chair and Shadow*, 1976, color lithograph,
24 x 17¾
signed *Kipniss* and *8/90*

13. *Reflections*, 1976, color lithograph, 20 x 15
signed *Kipniss* and *62/90*

14. *Afternoon*, 1976, color lithograph, 19⅞ x 15⅞
signed *Kipniss* and *7/90*

15. *Winter*, 1977, color lithograph, 17 x 12⅞
signed *Kipniss* and *xv/xx*
edition 100

16. *Hillside Place*, 1977, color lithograph, 19⅝ x 14⅜
signed *Kipniss* and *artist's proof, xv/xxv*

***17.** *Fields and Twilight*, 1977, color lithograph,
18 x 13⅞
signed *Kipniss* and *9/90*

***18.** *Leaves Aloft*, 1978, color lithograph, 16⅞ x 13⅞
signed *Kipniss* and *5/120*

19. *Green Roofs*, 1978, color lithograph, 16⅝ x 14¾
signed *Kipniss* and *5/120*

20. *Shadows II*, 1978, color lithograph, 16⅝ x 15¾
signed *Kipniss* and *5/120*

21. *Gateway*, 1978, color lithograph, 13⅞ x 13⅞
signed *Kipniss* and *artist's proof, viii/xxv*
edition 150

22. *Without, Within*, 1978, color lithograph, 24 x 18
signed *Kipniss* and *4/120*

23. *Secrets*, 1979, color lithograph, 15⅞ x 19⅞
signed *Kipniss* and *8/120*

24. *To Return*, 1980, color lithograph, 23½ x 18
signed *Kipniss* and *7/120*

25. *Reminiscences*, 1980, color lithograph, 23½ x 18
signed *Kipniss* and *artist's proof, viii/xxv*
edition 175

26. *Spring Secrets*, 1980, color lithograph, 19 x 24
signed *Kipniss* and *11/120*

27. *Window with Leaves*, 1980, color lithograph, 16 x 14
signed *Kipniss* and *11/120*

28. *Ohio Night*, 1981, color lithograph, 16¾ x 16
signed *Kipniss* and *9/120*

29. *Interlude*, 1981, color lithograph, 13 x 14
signed *Kipniss* and *artist's proof, xx/xxv*
edition 275

*30. *Shimmering Hedge*, 1982, color lithograph, 13½ x 10
signed *Kipniss* and *155/175*

*31. *Suspension*, 1982, color lithograph, 18 x 22
signed *Kipniss* and *28/120*

*32. *Picket Fences IV*, 1982, color lithograph, 13½ x 14
signed *Kipniss* and *151/175*

33. *Hillside Illusions*, 1982, color lithograph, 15 x 15½
signed *Kipniss* and *artist's proof, xix/xxx*
edition 250

34. *White Star*, 1982, color lithograph, 15 x 13
signed *Kipniss* and *28/120*

35. *Souvenirs*, 1982, color lithograph, 13½ x 10
signed *Kipniss* and *33/150*

36. *Studio Flowers*, 1982, color lithograph, 24 x 18
signed *Kipniss* and *28/120*

37. *Window with Orange Curtain*, 1987, color lithograph,
17½ x 14
signed *Kipniss* and *40/120*

38. *The Entrance*, 1983, color lithograph, 22 x 18
signed *Kipniss* and *13/120*

39. *A Private Porch*, 1984, color lithograph, 17 x 16
signed *Kipniss* and *2/120*

*40. *Interior with Yellow Flowers*, 1985, color lithograph,
17 x 15
signed *Kipniss and for James, with friendship,
Robert 9/14/85*
edition 120

41. *Just Before the Sun*, 1985, color lithograph, 12 x 11
signed *Kipniss* and *6/120*

*42. *Stairway*, 1985, color lithograph, 11 x 10
signed *Kipniss* and *9/120*

*43. Poised, 1986, color lithograph, 11 x 15
signed *Kipniss* and *2/120*

44. *Through Bedroom Curtains*, 1983, color lithograph,
20 x 18
signed *Kipniss* and *13/120*

45. *Streets and Alleys, Afternoon*, 1987, color lithograph,
11 x 12¾
signed *Kipniss* and *artist's proof*
edition 120

*46. *Green, Green*, 1987, color lithograph, 16 x 12
signed *Kipniss* and *2/120*

47. *The Blue Stove*, 987, color lithograph, 17½ x 14
signed *Kipniss* and *2/120*

*48. *Facades*, 1989, color lithograph, 14 x 14
signed *Kipniss* and *6/120*

49. *Eaves and Dark Windows*, 1989, color lithograph,
14 x 14
signed *Kipniss* and *6/120*

*50. *Interior w/large tree*, 1991, mezzotint, 5⅞ x 3⅝
signed *Kipniss* and *60/75*

51. *Sentinels*, 1992, mezzotint, 13⅞ x 9
signed *Kipniss* and *artist's proof, ii/x*

*52. *Rooftops & porch*, 1992, mezzotint, 7 x 6⅞
signed *Kipniss* and *55/60*

53. *Springfield, O.*, 1992, drypoint, 12 x 10⅞
signed *Kipniss, trial proof* and *for James White,
in friendship, 8.7.02*

54. *Backyards, evening*, 1995, mezzotint, 9⅜ x 7
signed *Kipniss* and *15/60*

55. *Clear vase & landscape*, 1995, mezzotint, 9⅜ x 14
signed *Kipniss* and *66/75*

56. *To the reservoir*, 1995, mezzotint, 9⅜ x 7
signed *Kipniss* and *21/40*

*57. *Vase, chair & trees*, 1995, mezzotint, 9⅜ x 7
signed *Kipniss* and *36/60*

58. *Alleys, Springfield*, 1995, mezzotint, 7 x 7⅞
signed *Kipniss* and *artist's proof, viii/x*

*59. *The black table*, 1995, mezzotint, 9⅜ x 7
  signed *Kipniss* and *artist's proof*

60. *August night*, 1996, mezzotint, 7⅞ x 7
  signed *Kipniss* and *9/60*

6l. *Easel & trees w/ moon*, 1996, mezzotint, 14 x 9⅜
  signed *Kipniss* and *22/60*

62. *Hillside shadows*, 1997, mezzotint, 11⅝ x 9⅜
  signed *Kipniss* and *artist's proof*

63. *Still life w/spoon*, 1998, mezzotint, 9⅜ x 11⅝
  signed *Kipniss* and *3/50*

64. *Sentinels II* (first state), 1998, mezzotint, 14 x 9⅜
  signed *Kipniss* and *14/50*

65. *For Stella*, 1998, mezzotint, 19 x 19
  signed *Kipniss* and *artist's proof*

66. *Still life w/kettle & cup*, 1998, mezzotint, 14 x 9⅜
  signed *Kipniss* and *14/50*

*67. *Fragments*, 1999, mezzotint, 14 x 9⅜
  signed *Kipniss* and *34/50*

68. *Houses & sheds*, 1999, mezzotint, 11⅝ x 9⅜
  signed *Kipniss* and *38/50*

69. *Vase w/small branches*, 1999, mezzotint, 9⅜ x 6
  signed *Kipniss* and *b.a.t.*

70. *Window w/bench & trees*, 1999, 19⅞ x 15⅝
  signed *Kipniss* and *39/60*

71. *Garden shadows*, 2000, mezzotint, 11⅝ x 9⅜
  signed *Kipniss* and *20/60*

72. *Forest nocturne III*, 2000, mezzotint, 14 x 9⅜
  signed *Kipniss* and *trial proof*

73. *Incandescence*, 2000, mezzotint, 7⅞ x 7
  signed *Kipniss* and *9/60*

74. *Window w/vase & forest*, 2000, mezzotint, 19½ x 19½
  signed *Kipniss* and *38/60*
  Collection of New Orleans Museum of Art: Gift of James F.
  White in honor of his parents, Agnes and Richard White,
  2002.217

75. *The white forest*, 2000, mezzotint, 23⅞ x 17
  signed *Kipniss* and *20/60*
  Collection of New Orleans Museum of Art: Gift of James F.
  White in honor of his parents, Agnes and Richard White,
  2002.221

76. *Crossings*, 2001, mezzotint, 11⅝ x 9⅜
  signed *Kipniss* and *9/60*
  Collection of New Orleans Museum of Art: Gift of James F.
  White in honor of his parents, Agnes and Richard White,
  2002.219

77. *Tall trees at night*, 2001, mezzotint, 19⅝ x 13
  signed *Kipniss* and *34/60*
  Collection of New Orleans Museum of Art: Gift of James F.
  White in honor of his parents, Agnes and Richard White,
  2002.218

78. *Forest nocturne IV*, 2001, mezzotint, 19⅜ x 14
  signed *Kipniss* and *artist's proof, vi/x*
  Collection of New Orleans Museum of Art: Gift of James F.
  White in honor of his parents, Agnes and Richard White,
  2002.220

79. *Still life w/dark window*, 2001, mezzotint, 14 x 9⅜
  signed *Kipniss* and *trial proof*

80. *Illuminata*, 2001, mezzotint, 7⅞ x 7
  signed *Kipniss* and *artist's proof, xvi/xx*

*81. *Rooftops, Lakeville*, 2002, mezzotint, 9 x 6
  signed *Kipniss* and *artist's proof*

82. *Still life w/chair & standing lamp*, 2002, mezzotint,
  11⅝ x 9⅜
  signed *Kipniss* and *12/60*

83. *Interior w/cup, spoon & window*, 2003, mezzotint, 7 x 5
  signed *Kipniss* and *artist's proof, i/xii*

84. *Two vases*, 2004, mezzotint, 19½ x 15⅜
  signed *Kipniss* and *artist's proof, ix/xiii*

85. *The balanced rock*, 2004, mezzotint, 19½ x 19⅜
  signed *Kipniss* and *artist's proof, iv/xv*

86. *Nocturne: still life w/two vases*, 2004, mezzotint,
  19½ x 13
  signed *Kipniss* and *74/75*

Selected Public Collections

(PAINTINGS, PRINTS, DRAWINGS)

Achenbach Foundation for Graphic Arts, The Fine Arts Museums of San Francisco, California Palace of the Legion of Honor

Albright-Knox Art Gallery, Buffalo, New York

Allentown Art Museum, Allentown, Pennsylvania

Arkansas State University Permanent Collection, State University, Arkansas

The Art Institute of Chicago, Chicago, Illinois

Art Museum of Western Virginia, Roanoke, Virginia

Art Students League of New York, New York

Ball State University, Muncie, Indiana

Bates College Museum of Art, Lewiston, Maine

Bibliotheque nationale de France, Paris

Bodleian Library, Oxford University, Oxford, England

The British Museum, London

Brooklyn Museum of Art, Brooklyn, New York

The Butler Institute of American Art, Youngstown, Ohio

Canton Art Institute, Canton, Ohio

Carnegie Museum of Art, Pittsburgh, Pennsylvania

The Century Association, New York, New York

The Cleveland Museum of Art, Cleveland, Ohio

Davis Museum and Cultural Center, Wellesley College, Wellesley, Massachusetts

De Cordova Museum and Sculpture Park, Lincoln, Massachusetts

Denver Art Museum, Denver, Colorado

The Detroit Institute of Arts, Detroit, Michigan

Dubuque Museum of Art, Dubuque, Iowa

Elvehjem Museum of Art, University of Wisconsin-Madison, Wisconsin

Everson Museum of Art, Syracuse, New York

Fitzwilliam Museum, University of Cambridge, Cambridge, UK

Flint Institute of Arts, Flint, Michigan

Frederick R. Weisman Art Museum, University of Minnesota, Minneapolis

Gibbes Museum of Art, Charleston, South Carolina

Harvard University Art Museums, Cambridge, Massachusetts

The Herbert F. Johnson Museum of Art, Cornell University, Ithaca, New York

Indianapolis Museum of Art, Indianapolis, Indiana

Iris & B. Gerald Cantor Center for Visual Arts at Stanford University, Stanford, California

Jane Voorhees Zimmerli Art Museum, Rutgers, The State University of New Jersey, New Brunswick

Lakeview Museum of Arts and Sciences, Peoria, Illinois

Library of Congress, Washington, D.C.

Los Angeles County Museum of Art, Los Angeles, California

The Marion Koogler McNay Art Museum, San Antonio, Texas

The Metropolitan Museum of Art, New York, New York

Miami University Art Museum, Oxford, Ohio

Minnesota Museum of American Art, Saint Paul, Minnesota

Mint Museum of Art, Charlotte, North Carolina

Mississippi Museum of Art, Jackson, Mississippi

Museo de Arte Moderno La Tertulia, Cali, Colombia

Museum of Art, Rhode Island School of Design, Providence

Museum of Fine Arts, Boston, Massachusetts

The Museum of Fine Arts, Houston, Texas

National Academy of Design, New York, New York

National Museum of American Art, Washington, D.C.

The Nelson-Atkins Museum of Art, Kansas City, Missouri

New Orleans Museum of Art, New Orleans, Louisiana

The New York Public Library, Print Collection, New York, New York

Notre Dame University, South Bend, Indiana

Ohio University, Athens, Ohio

Orlando Museum of Art, Orlando, Florida

Pennsylvania State University Library Collection, State College, Pennsylvania

Philadelphia Museum of Art, Philadelphia, Pennsylvania

Pinakothek der Moderne, Staatliche Graphische Sammlung, Munich

Portland Art Museum, Portland, Oregon

Print Club of Albany, Albany, New York

Royal Society of Painter-Printmakers, London (diploma piece); housed at the Ashmolean Museum, Oxford

Society of American Graphic Artists (SAGA), New York, New York

Southern Alleghenies Museum of Art, Loretto, Pennsylvania

Springfield Art Museum, Springfield, Missouri

Springfield Museum of Art, Springfield, Ohio

Tacoma Art Museum, Tacoma, Washington

Victoria and Albert Museum, London

Virginia Museum of Fine Arts, Richmond, Virginia

Wellesley College, Wellesley, Massachusetts

Whitney Museum of American Art, New York, New York

Wichita Falls Museum and Art Center, Wichita Falls, Texas

Wittenberg University, Springfield, Ohio

Yale University Art Gallery, New Haven, Connecticut

Selected Solo Exhibitions

(PAINTINGS, PRINTS, DRAWINGS)

The Old Print Shop, New York, New York, 2004

SKH Gallery, Great Barrington, Massachusetts, 2004

Springfield Art Museum, Springfield, Missouri, 2003

Beadleston Gallery, New York, New York, 2003, 2001

Wichita Falls Museum and Art Center, Wichita Falls, Texas, 2003

(A retrospective of paintings and graphics, 1950s-1990s), 1997

Harmon-Meek Gallery, Naples, Florida, 2002

Weinstein Gallery, San Francisco, California, 2002, 2001, 2000

Galerie Gerda Bassenge, Berlin, Germany, 1999

The Butler Institute of American Art, Youngstown, Ohio, 1999

Tyler Museum of Art, Tyler, Texas, 1999

Gerhard Wurzer Gallery, Houston, Texas, 1999, 1997, 1988, 1986, 1981

Molesey Gallery, East Molesey, Surrey, UK, 1999, 1995

Redfern Gallery, London, 1999, 1995

Davidson Gallery, Seattle, Washington, 1999, 1993, 1983, 1982

Gallery M, Denver, Colorado, 1999

Gallery New World, Düsseldorf, Germany, 1998, 1995

Jane Haslem Gallery, Washington, D.C., 1998, 1976

Hexton Gallery, New York, New York, 1997, 1996, 1995, 1994

Venable/Neslage Gallery, Washington, D.C., 1997, 1995

The Century Association, New York, New York, 1996

Taunhaus Gallery, Osaka and Kanazawa, Japan, 1994

Laura Craig Gallery, Scranton, Pennsylvania, 1993, 1991, 1990

Wittenberg University, Springfield, Ohio, 1993, 1979

Theodore B. Donson Gallery, New York, New York, 1992

River Gallery, Irvington-on-Hudson, New York, 1991

OK Harris Works of Art, New York, New York, 1991

Enatsu Gallery, Tokyo, Japan, 1990, 1988, 1987

Illinois College, Jacksonville, Illinois, 1989

Robert Urban Gallery, Baltimore, Maryland, 1987

Jamie Szoke Gallery, New York, New York, 1985

Summa Gallery, New York, New York, 1985

Haller-Griffin Gallery, Washington Depot, Connecticut, 1985

Austin Gallery, Scottsdale, Arizona, 1985, 1985

Springfield Museum of Art, Springfield, Ohio, 1985, 1983

Nancy Teague Gallery, Seattle, Washington, 1983, 1982

ICA, Nagoya, Japan, 1984

Payson/Weisberg Gallery, New York, New York, 1983, 1981

Bruce Museum of Arts and Science, Greenwich, Connecticut, 1981

Gage Gallery, Washington, D.C., 1983, 1981

Hirschl & Adler Galleries, New York, New York, 1980, 1977

Museo de Arte Moderno La Tertulia, Cab,
    Colombia, 1980, 1975
Canton Art Institute, Canton, Ohio, 1979
Associated American Artists , New York, New York,
    1977 (ten-year lithography retrospective)
G.W. Einstein Gallery, 1976, 1977
Galeriá de Arte, Lima, Peru, 1977
Galeriá San Diego, Bogota, Colombia, 1977,
    1975
Centro de Arte Actual, Pereira, Colombia, 1975
Kalamazoo Institute of Arts, Kalamazoo, Michigan,
    1975
Xochipili Gallery, Rochester, Michigan, 1975

FAR Gallery, New York, New York, 1975, 1972,
    1970, 1968
The Contemporaries, New York, New York, 1967,
    1966, 1960, 1959
Allen R. Hite Institute, University of Louisville,
    Kentucky, 1965
Gallery Vendome, Pittsburgh, Pennsylvania, 1965
Alan Auslander Gallery, New York, New York,
    1963
Harry Salpeter Gallery, New York, New York, 1953
Joe Gans Gallery, New York, New York, 1951

SELECTED GROUP
EXHIBITIONS

The Jane Voorhees Zimmerli Art Museum, Rutgers University, The State of New Jersey, New Brunswick, *The Color of Night*, 2005

The Berkshire Museum, Pittsfield, Massachusetts, *The Power of Place: The Berkshires*, 2005

The Forbes Galleries, New York, New York, *"A Record of What Has Been Accomplished": Highights from the Permanent Collection of the Art Students League of New York*, 2004

Everson Museum of Art, Syracuse, New York, *Object Lessons:Additions to the Collection, 1997-2002*, 2003

Orlando Museum of Art, Orlando, Florida, *Celebrating a Decade of Growth: Selections from the Orlando Museum of Art's Permanent Collections*, 2003

Tacoma Art Museum, Tacoma, Washington, *Pressed: Intaglio*, 2002

USB PaineWebber Art Gallery, New York, New York, *A Century on Paper*, 2002

Art Museum of Western Virginia, Roanoke, Virginia, *Selected Recent Acquisitions, 2002*

New Orleans Museum of Art, New Orleans, Louisiana, *Acquisitions in Prints and Drawings, 1996-2000*, 2001

The British Museum, London, *Recent Acquisitions*, 2000

National Academy of Design, New York, New York, *Treasures Revealed: Nineteenth- and Twentieth- Century American Works on Paper*, 1999

Fitzwilliam Museum, University of Cambridge, Cambridge, UK, *Recent Acquisitions*, 1999

Ashmolean Museum, Oxford, *No Day Without A Line*, Diploma Prints of the Royal Society of Painter-Printmakers, London, 1999

Light and Shadow: The Changing Seasons, Lizan-Tops Gallery, East Hampton, New York, 1995

American Academy of Arts and Letters, New York, New York, *Invitational Exhibition*, 1988

Tahir Gallery, New Orleans, Louisiana, *American Self Portraits*, 1981

Museo de Arte Moderno La Tertulia, Cali, Colombia, S.A.,*Grabadores Norteamericonos*, 1978

III Bienal Americana de Artes Graficas, Museo La Tertulia, Cali, Colombia, S.A., 1976

International Exhibition of Original Drawings, Rijeka-Dolac, Yugoslavia, 1976

Kalamazoo Art Institute, Kalamazoo, Michigan, 1975

Westmoreland Museum, Pittsburgh, Pennsylvania, 1974, 1973, 1972

Whitney Museum of American Art, New York, New York, *Recent Acquisitions*, 1972

American Federation of Arts traveling exhibition *Moods of Light*, 1963-1965:
Vanderbilt Gallery, Nashville, Tennessee
Andrew Dickson White Museum, Cornell University, Ithica, New York
Davenport Municipal Art Gallery, Davenport, Iowa
Utah Museum of Fine Arts, Salt Lake City, Utah
University of Manitoba, Winnipeg, Manitoba, Canada
West Virginia University, Morgantown, West Virginia

Cranbrook Academy of Art, Bloomfield Hills, Michigan
Paul Sargent Gallery, Eastern Illinois University, Charlestown, Illinois
Nordness Gallery, New York, New York, *The Artist Depicts the Artist*, 1961
The Sheldon Swope Gallery, Terre Haute, Indiana, 1961
Art in America, New York, New York, 1961
Tweed Gallery, University of Minnesota, Duluth, Minnesota, *Contemporary Artists*, 1962

Osborne Gallery, New York, New York, *The Contemporary American Landscape*, 1963
Graham Gallery, New York, New York, *East Coast Landscape*, 1964
Herron Museum of Art, Indianapolis, Indiana, *Painting & Sculpture Today*, 1964
The Columbus Museum of Art, Columbus, Ohio, 1957
The Massillon Museum, Ohio, 1957
Butler Art Institute of Art, Youngstown, Ohio 1953

Selected Bibliography

PERIODICALS AND NEWSPAPERS

Ashton, Dore. "Suggestions of Romance," *The Art Digest* 26, 1 (October, 1951): 20

_____. untitled exhibition review, *The New York Times* (November, 1959).

Campbell, Lawrence. untitled exhibition review, *ARTnews* 52, 6 (October , 1953): 56.

Carter, Richard. "On Display: Robert Kipniss' Mezzotints," *Times Record News*, Wichita Falls, Texas(September 19, 2003), illustration.

Caldwell, John. "Kipniss Lends Vision to Realist School," *The New York Times* (October 10, 1982), illustration: 28.

Conner, Alice Ann. "Detail Work," *Kenosha News* (January 3l-February 7, 1997), illustration: 8.

C.B. "Kipniss Art Show," *New York Herald Tribune* (December 5, 1959).

_____. untitled exhibition review, *Arts* (January, 1960).

_____. untitled exhibition review, *New York Herald Tribune* (December 10, 1960).

_____. untitled exhibition review, *The New York Times* (December 11, 1960).

_____. untitled exhibition review, *New York Herald Tribune* (October 19, 1963).

_____. untitled exhibition review, *The New York Times* (November 2, 1963).

Dahl, Renee. untitled exhibition review, *ArtBeat: East Hampton Independent* (October 18, 1995), illustrations: 52.

Dumas, Carol K. "Inner Landscapes," *The Cape Codder* (August 5, 1994), illustrations: 24.

Farber, Howard. "Robert Kipniss' poetry of form and feeling," *Artspeak* (October 1, 1989), illustration: 7.

Genauer, Emily. untitled exhibition review, *New York Herald Tribune* (September 19, 1953).

_____.untitled exhibition review, *The New York Times* (September 19, 1953).

Genauer, Emily and John Gruen. "Friday Tour of Art," *World Journal Tribune* (New York, January 13, 1967): 38.

Gruen, John. untitled exhibition review, *New York Herald Tribune* (January 29, 1966).

_____: untitled exhibition review, *The New York Times* (January 29, 1966).

_____: untitled exhibition review, *Time* 87, 5 (February 4, 1966): E2.

_____: untitled exhibition review, *Art International* X/4 (April, 1966), illustration: 82-83

Lunde, Karl. "Robert Kipniss," *Arts Magazine* (May 1977), illustration: 8.

Lunde, Karl. "Robert Kipniss," *Arts Magazine* (February l979), illustration: 15.

McCormack, Ed. "The Tranquil Intensity of Robert Kipniss," *Artspeak* (April 1, 1989), illustration: 1.

_____. "Robert Kipniss: A Draftsman's Mastery," *Artspeak* (November 1997), illustration.

_____. "Kipniss Drawings Begin Run at TMA," *Tyler Morning Telegraph* sec. 6 (November 19, 1999), illustration: 8.

Mikotajuk, Andrea. untitled exhibition review, *Arts Magazine* (December-January, 1973): 91.

Miller, Marlan. "Austin Gallery Exhibit Theme is Landscape," *The Phoenix Gazette Marquee*, Phoenix, Arizona (June 26, 1l976), illustation.

_____. "Gallery of Landscapes Soothing to the Eyes," *The Phoenix Gazette Marquee*, Phoenix, Arizona (July 7, 1979), illustration.

Monagan, Bill. "In a Different Light," *Springfield News-Sun*, Springfield, Ohio (October 11, 1987), illustration: 1-2B.

Parsons, Martin. "A major Robert Kipniss exhibition at Hexton Gallery," *Artspeak* (December 1994), illustration: 12.

Pyne, Lynn. "Paintings depict artist's feelings," *The Phoenix Gazette Marquee*, Phoenix, Arizona (March 23, 1983): illustrations: NE6, NE13.

Steiner, Raymond J. "Kipniss at River Gallery," *Art Times* (December, 1991), illustration: 8.

Wepman, Dennis. "The inner eye of Robert Kipniss," *Artspeak* (November 1, 1986), illustration: 11.

BOOKS AND EXHIBITION CATALOGUES

Allen, Philip. *Robert Kipniss: Intaglio and Oil*, Weinstein Gallery, San Francisco, California, 2004.

Beadleston Gallery, New York, New York, *Robert Kipniss: Paintings and Drawings*, 2001.

Beadleston Gallery, New York, New York, *Robert Kipniss*, 2003.

Cox, Richard. *American Self Portraits*, Tahir Gallery, New Orleans, Louisiana, 1981

FAR Gallery, New York, New York, *Robert Kipniss: Recent Paintings*, 1968.

Galerie Gerda Bassenge, Berlin, *Robert Kipniss: Mezzotints and Lithographs*, 1999

Gerhard Wurzer Gallery, Houston, *Transitions: Drawings 1960-64/Robert Kipniss*, Texas, 1999.

Grace, Trudie A. *Paper Trail: Prints, Drawings and Watercolors in the National Academy of Design*, National Academy of Design, New York, New York, 2000

Grace, Trudie A. and Thomas Piche, Jr. *Robert Kipniss: Intaglios 1982-2004*, Hudson Hills Press, New York, New York, 2004 (awarded bronze medal for art book of the year by Foreword Magazine).

Harmon-Meek Gallery, Naples, Florida, 1999.

Lunde, Karl. *Robert Kipniss: Recent Paintings*, Hirschl & Adler Galleries, Inc., New York, 1980.

_____. *Robert Kipniss: The Graphic Work*, Abaris Books, New York, New York, 1980.

Mc Cormack, Ed. *Robert Kipniss: Taking Time*, Weinstein Gallery, San Francisco, California, 2001.

Springfield Art Center, Springfield, Ohio, *Robert Kipniss: Inner Landscapes*, 1981.

Theodore B. Donson Gallery, New York, New York, *Robert Kipniss: Drypoints and Mezzotints*, 1992.

Weinstein Gallery, San Francisco, California, *Robert Kipniss: Painter/Printmaker*, 2000.

Weinstein Gallery, San Francisco, California, *Robert Kipniss: Lithographs from the Artist's Archives, 1968-1990*, 2002.

Wichita Falls Museum & Art Center, Wichita Falls, Texas, *Robert Kipniss: The Image and the Medium*, 1997.

whale

scorpion fish

ferry

jellyfish

submersible

seal

lighthouse

butterfly fish

seaweed

Ocean

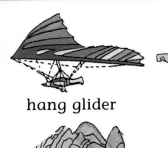

hang glider

rocks

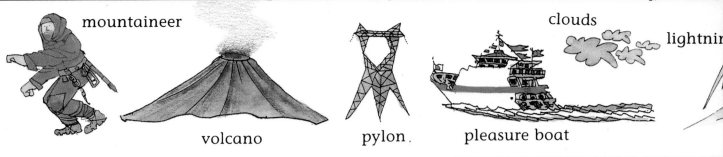

mountaineer

volcano

pylon

clouds

pleasure boat

lightnin

mountain

rain

dam

fir trees

rainbow

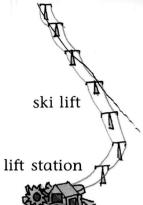

ski lift

lift station

Mountains

monkey

rhinoceros

leopard

wildcat

hawk

armadillo

snake

chameleon

butterfly

tiger

vine   macaw   trees   kingfisher   leaves   insect   lemur   flower   heron   toucan

Jungle

house

church

pedestrian crossing

fire engine

bicycle

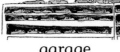

garage

bus

motorcycle

satellite dish

dome

door

bulldozer

tower

lamp post

theater

clock

car

steps

store

telephone
booth

cement mixer
truck

pickup truck

Town

space shuttle

steam
locomotive

jet fighter

cargo ship

racing car

Chinese junk

hansom cab

diesel-electric locomotive

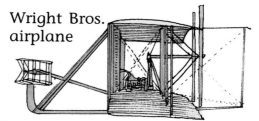
Wright Bros.
airplane

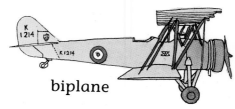
biplane

galleon

vintage car

Transportation

balloons

owl

ice cream

egg

rabbit

apples cherries potatoes

cabbages

toy alphabet

clothes

sausages

cat carrots corn-on-the-cob artichokes tomatoes pears grapes beans

flowers

shoes

toys

Market

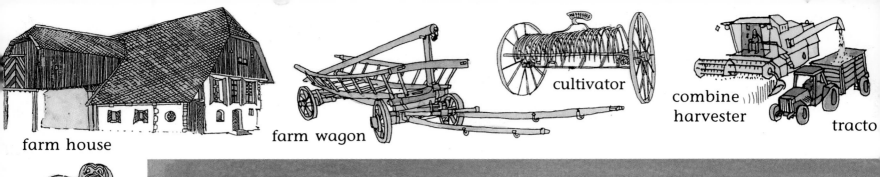

farm house

farm wagon

cultivator

combine harvester

tractor

dog

horse

cow

wasp

farmer

barn

quilt

goose

turkey

cat

well

rooster

kennel

milk cans

watering can

quail

Farm

elephant

stork

leopard

buffalo

hippopotamus

gazelle

zebra

yak

musk ox

own bear

peacock

cheetah

giraffe

moose

deer

raccoon

kangaroo

gnu

ostrich

llama

lion

pelican

Wildlife Park

Brachiosaurus

Tyrannosaurus
rex

Allosaurus

Ankylosaurus

Deinonychus

Triceratops

Torosaurus

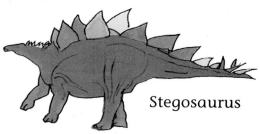

Stegosaurus

Corythosaurus

Ouranosaurus

Iguanodon

Dinosaurs

narrator

Puss-in-Boots

wizard

doll

queen king wand fairy

baby

cradle

monster

curtain

dragon

xylophone

cello

violin

clarinet

soldier

mother

School Play

slide

children

seesaw

yellow star

turquoise circle

white square

climbing ropes

jungle gym

 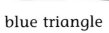
orange zigzag

blue triangle

pink rectangle

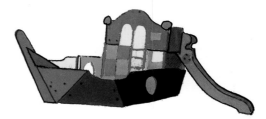
play boat

red ladder

blue spiral

orange stripes

red heart

Playground

Index

Index

rectangle PLAYGROUND
red heart PLAYGROUND
red ladder PLAYGROUND
rhinoceros JUNGLE
rocks MOUNTAINS
rooster FARMS

satellite SPACE
satellite dish TOWN
sausages MARKET
scorpion DESERT
scorpion fish OCEAN
sea horse OCEAN
seagull OCEAN
seal OCEAN
seaweed OCEAN
seesaw PLAYGROUND
shark OCEAN
shell OCEAN
shoes MARKET
shooting star SPACE
ski lift MOUNTAINS
slide PLAYGROUND
snake JUNGLE
soldier SCHOOL PLAY
space capsule SPACE
spaceship SPACE
space shuttle TRANSPORTATION
sphinx DESERT

spiral PLAYGROUND
square PLAYGROUND
star PLAYGROUND
steam locomotive TRANSPORTATION
store TOWN
Stegosaurus DINOSAURS
steps TOWN
stork WILDLIFE PARK
stripes PLAYGROUND
submarine OCEAN
submersible OCEAN
sun SPACE

telephone booth TOWN
tent DESERT
theater TOWN
tiger JUNGLE
tomatoes MARKET
Torosaurus DINOSAURS
toucan JUNGLE
tower TOWN
toy alphabet MARKET
toys MARKET
tractor FARM
trees JUNGLE
triangle PLAYGROUND
Triceratops DINOSAURS
truck TOWN
turkey FARM

turquoise circle PLAYGROUND
Tyrannosaurus rex
    DINOSAURS

veil DESERT
vine JUNGLE
vintage car TRANSPORTATION
violin SCHOOL PLAY
volcano MOUNTAINS

wand SCHOOL PLAY
wasp FARM
water jar DESERT
watering can FARM
well FARM
whale OCEAN
white square PLAYGROUND
wildcat JUNGLE
wizard SCHOOL PLAY
Wright Bros. airplane
    TRANSPORTATION

xylophone SCHOOL PLAY

yak WILDLIFE PARK
yellow star PLAYGROUND

zebra WILDLIFE PARK
zigzag PLAYGROUND

There are many more amazing objects in each picture.
Can you find some of these?

DESERT
antenna
cushion
hawk
Rolls Royce
sand dune
shawl
walking stick

OCEAN
cliff
fishing line
hammerhead shark
lobster
ship wreck
turtle

MOUNTAINS
beaver
deer
eagle
fire
lake
waterfall

JUNGLE
eagle
owl

TOWN
antenna
bucket
cat
backhoe
dog
fork
pick
pipe
shovel
flatbed truck

TRANSPORTATION
steam locomotive
radio telescope
sailing boat
triplane
vintage tractor

MARKET
chicken

crate
doll's house
flower pot
shopping basket
tablecloth
toy car
toy train
umbrella
vase

FARM
baler
barrel
bucket
chicken
ladder
pitchfork
sack
wheel
wheelbarrow

WILDLIFE PARK
armadillo
lioness
polar bear

stork
tiger

DINOSAURS
camel skeleton
columns
flying Pterosaurus
gorilla skeleton

SCHOOL PLAY
alphabet
battlement
boots
cloud
crown
hat
horse
moon
mustache
old record player
sun
tree

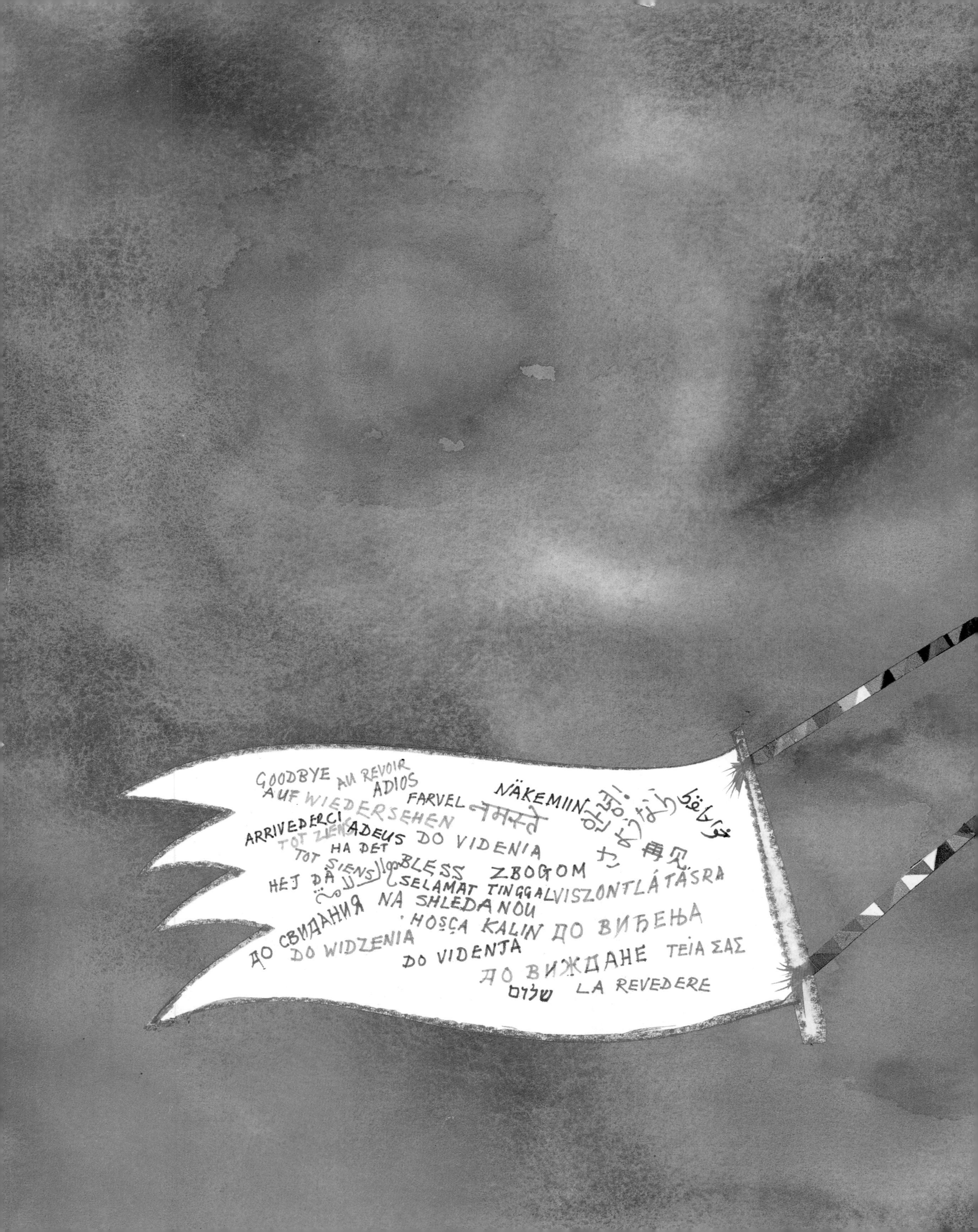
GOODBYE
AU REVOIR
ADIOS
AUF WIEDERSEHEN
FARVEL
नमस्ते
NÄKEMIIN
안녕!
ARRIVEDERCI
TOT ZIENS
ADEUS
DO VIDENIA
HA DET
再见
TOT SIENS
BLESS
ZBOGOM
HEJ DÅ
SELAMAT TINGGAL
VISZONTLÁTÁSRA
ДО СВИДАНИЯ
NA SHLEDANOU
HOŞÇA KALIN
ДО ВИЂЕЊА
DO WIDZENIA
DO VIDENJA
ДО ВИЖДАНЕ
ΓΕΙΑ ΣΑΣ
שלום
LA REVEDERE

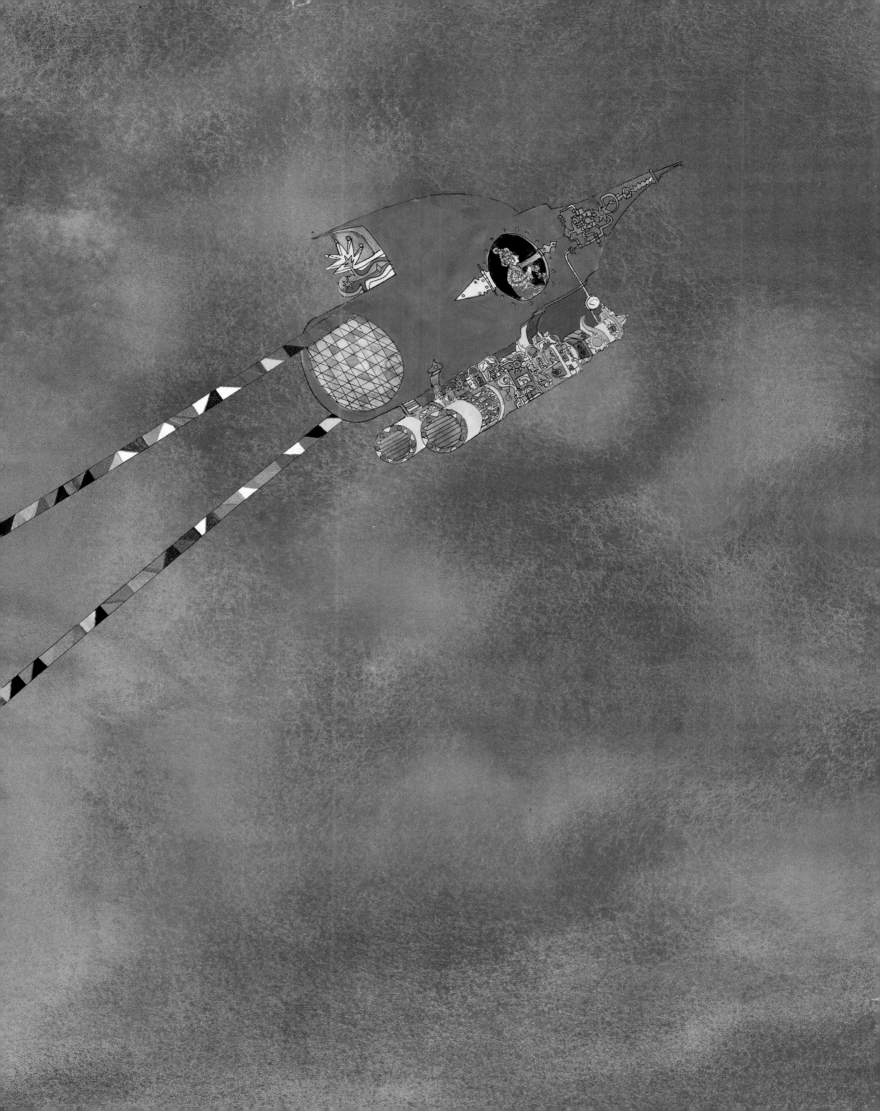